Dining on the Oregon Coast

Restaurants & Recipes

Steve and Mary Taylor

Printed by:
Poverty Bay Publishing Company

Published by Poverty Bay Publishing Co.
529 S.W. 294th Ave.
Federal Way, WA 98003
Cover Photography: Jerome Hart
Cover Design: Coates Creates and the authors
Manufactured in the United States

ISBN 0-936528-00-1
Library of Congress Catalog Card Number 78-057748

Contents

TO HIERONYMUS
FOR PATIENCE AND TOLERANCE

AND TO FAMILY AND FRIENDS
WHO HELPED ALONG THE WAY . . .

OUR HUMBLE THANKS.

"I look upon it, that he who does not mind his belly will hardly mind anything else."

Samuel Johnson

THERE is an element of magic in the Oregon coast. There is a magic in the changing seasons and in the rugged, yet diverse, scenery that stretches from the mighty Columbia River south to the California border. There is magic in the abundant wildlife, whether it be the magnificent elk and deer of the forests; the plentiful and playful otters, seals and sea lions; the myriad breeds of bird life ranging from gulls to ospreys; or the fish that teem in coastal waters. And there is magic in the culinary experiences available to the discriminating diner who is willing to seek out a memorable meal.

It is to this latter style of magic that we dedicate this book, for we ourselves are committed to fine dining as a just reward for the hard labors of our hurry-scurry, work-a-day world. To partake of an expertly prepared meal in pleasant surroundings with someone you enjoy is to stop and smell the roses: you owe it to yourself—you earned it.

The Oregon coast, so bountiful in other rewards, is a mecca for those who truly appreciate the unique in dining. Seafoods are, of course, the specialty, but that should not imply limitation, for the fare is as diverse as it is delectable. In season the shellfish alone will have you in a quandary of indecision, with several varieties of clams, scallops, shrimp, oysters, and crab to tempt your palate. If you prefer your fish with fins, there's no need to worry. The Oregon coast has a plethora of species from which to choose. The fabled chinook salmon is certainly the all-time favorite, but don't overlook the halibut, red snapper, sea bass, sole, sturgeon, cod, trout, and other varieties as viable—and delicious—alternatives. If you're the rugged sportsman type, ready to go after your own via digging, raking, netting, or angling, so much the better; the experience of catching your meal can only enhance the dining pleasure. There are countless opportunities everywhere you look.

For us, the Oregon coast is the place we always "go back to;" the place where we recharge our batteries and regain our perspective. Over the years, we have spent a great deal of time on the coast looking for the out-of-the-way places as well as those more generally known, to sample and feast on the fare.

The restaurants included in this book are our favorites up and down the coast and were chosen strictly on the basis of merit. The common denominator was excellence. Yet, there is a great diversity among them. Each has its own special personality and pluses and ably serves the needs of a divergent resident and tourist clientele. While we make no attempt at critical evaluation, we feel confident that you can patronize any of the establishments and expect a quality meal. "Fast food" outlets have not been noted, as they are relatively consistent and well known, for better or worse. Rather, the focus here is primarily on dinner houses, the places you'll remember for months afterwards, places that helped make your stay on the coast more memorable. We accept no advertising; no restaurant can simply "buy its way in" to our book. To allow this would compromise its integrity.

In spite of a tradition of quality, it must be acknowledged that all restaurants occasionally have "off nights." It's for this reason that we haven't chosen to critically evaluate. The Bouillabaise that was so outstanding the night we were there might not be quite so good when you visit them, or vice versa. Tastes vary. The touch of an unfamiliar spice might be a delightful surprise to some and a disappointment to others.

The important thing to remember is that these are serious businesses which have earned the respect of a loyal clientele as well as a widespread reputation for excellence. They are characterized by a dedication to quality and individuality. We have personally patronized all of the restaurants and recommend them without hesitation to you as we would to a close personal friend.

A word about the menus: those printed were in existence at the time of publication. The items shown are subject to change. It goes without saying that the dishes offered by each restaurant will change at times, due as much to the imagination of the chef as to the seasonal availability. These menus then are primarily intended for use as a general guideline to the types of dishes offered. Given the current economic "norm" of rapid inflation we have not included actual prices from the menus. No restaurant owner increases his prices frivolously, but the unfortunate cost pressures of food prices, energy costs, higher wages and taxes makes occasional price increases unavoidable.

We are particularly excited by the recipes submitted by each of the restaurants. These are presented for those quiet, intimate evenings, when "dining in" is more your style. The recipes have been printed with very little editing so as to retain as much of the original chef's magic as possible. Augmenting them is the last section of the book, which contains a substantial number of additional recipes from the restaurants, as well as many of our own personal favorite recipes, accumulated and developed over the years. We sincerely hope that your dining experiences on the coast will motivate the more adventurous side of your personality to try some of these delicacies in your own home. You'll be well rewarded.

We're confident that you will be as captivated by this beautiful region of Oregon as we are. And we hope that *Dining on the Oregon Coast* will help to maximize your enjoyment of the many dining delights awaiting there.

The Restaurants

"All human history attests
that happiness for man,—the hungry sinner!—
Since Eve ate apples, much depends on dinner."

Byron

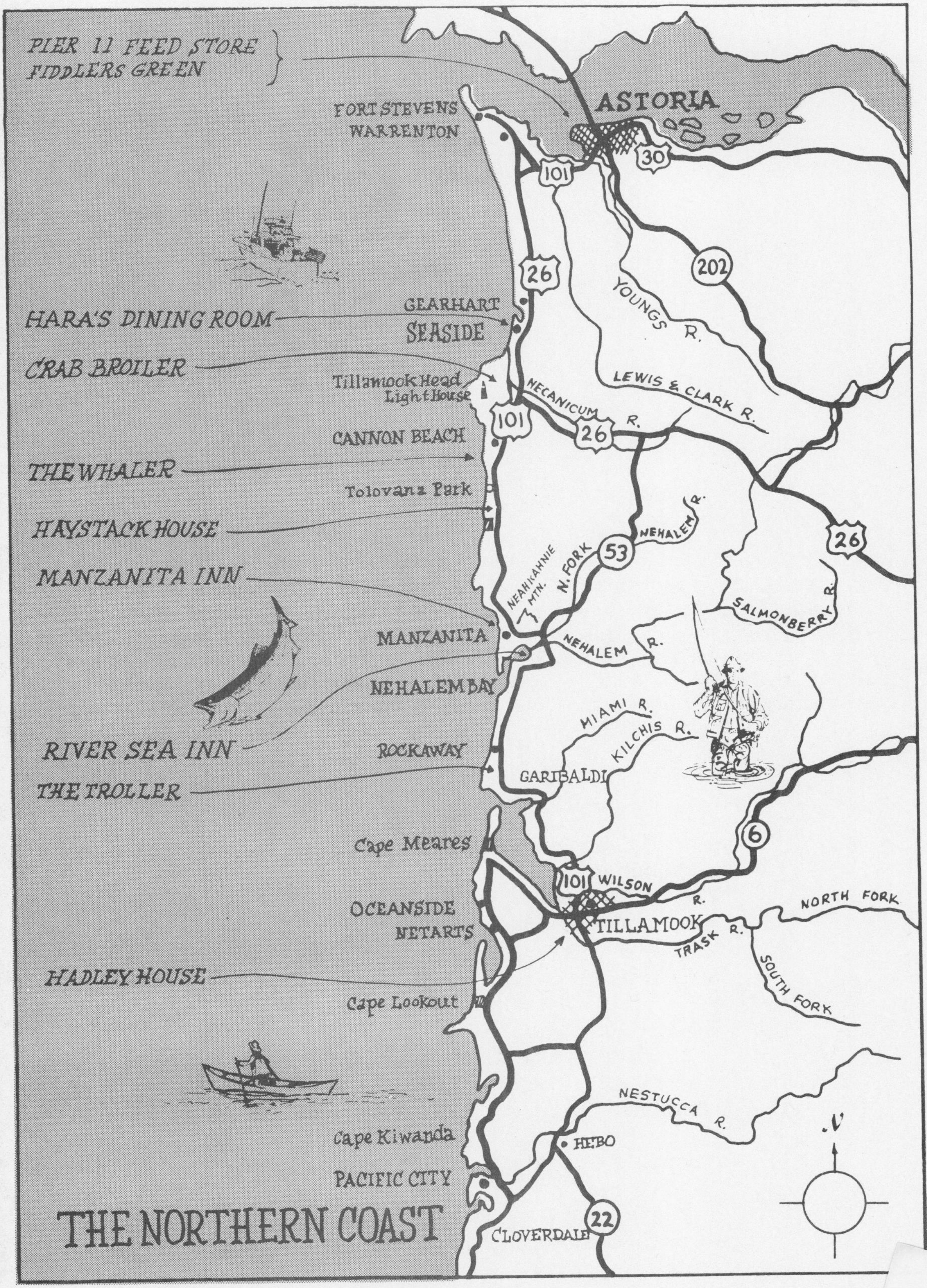
PIER 11 FEED STORE
FIDDLERS GREEN
ASTORIA
FORT STEVENS
WARRENTON
101
30
26
202
YOUNGS R.
GEARHART
HARA'S DINING ROOM
SEASIDE
CRAB BROILER
Tillamook Head
Light House
LEWIS & CLARK R.
NECANICUM R.
101
26
CANNON BEACH
THE WHALER
Tolovana Park
HAYSTACK HOUSE
NEHALEM R.
53
26
MANZANITA INN
NEAHKAHNIE MTN.
N. FORK
SALMONBERRY R.
MANZANITA
NEHALEM R.
NEHALEM BAY
MIAMI R.
KILCHIS R.
RIVER SEA INN
ROCKAWAY
THE TROLLER
GARIBALDI
6
Cape Meares
101
WILSON R.
NORTH FORK
OCEANSIDE
NETARTS
TILLAMOOK
TRASK R.
SOUTH FORK
HADLEY HOUSE
Cape Lookout
NESTUCCA R.
N
Cape Kiwanda
HEBO
PACIFIC CITY
22
THE NORTHERN COAST
CLOVERDALE

ORIGINALLY a freight depot, Pier 11 later was converted into a feed mill and store, and most recently into an assortment of shops and the Feed Store Restaurant and Lounge. The old beam ceiling has been retained, some walls are rough-sawn redwood while others are glassed, exposing the adjacent shops on one side and the Columbia River on the other. Owners Bill and Madonna Pittman host their customers amidst custom furnishings and treat them to the sights of seals frolicking and heavy river traffic. This uncommon view, the contemporary yet historic environs, and diverse menu all make for a memorable occasion.

Pier 11 Feed Store Restaurant and Lounge
77 11th Street
Astoria, OR 97103

325-0279

Hours: 11 am-10 pm daily
Closed Christmas

Libations: Full wine list, cocktails, and beer

Payment: VISA, Mastercharge, and personal checks

Reservations: Accepted in winter months only

Pier 11
Peppered Rib Eye

5-6 pound roast
½ cup cracked pepper
½ teaspoon ground cardamon
1 tablespoon paprika
½ teaspoon garlic powder
1 cup soy sauce
¾ cup wine vinegar
1 tablespoon tomato paste

Combine pepper and cardamon, rub over meat, and press into meat. Combine remaining ingredients and carefully pour over meat. Marinate at least overnight. Longer if possible. Wrap meat in foil and bake at 300°F. for 2 hours for medium rare.

You are Invited to Enjoy Dining at **Pier 11** FEED STORE Restaurant and Lounge

Family Style Service

Includes Soup or Salad, Rice Pilaf or Baked Potato, Bread, and Coffee, Tea or Sanka

CIOPPINO, A Fisherman's Stew - Delightful Combination of Fish and Shellfish in a Robust Tomato Sauce, Serves Two . . . .

OYSTER FEED, Willapa and Pacific Oysters Both Deep Fried and a La Natural, Served with a Hangtown Style Crepe for Real Oyster Lovers, Serves Two . . . .

VEAL HONGORISE, JUMBO PRAWNS, MUSHROOM CREPES, Our Gourmet Collection Dinner, Serves Two . . . .

CHICKEN KIEV, LANGOSTINO AND MUSHROOM CREPES, Our Ideal Combination for Your Dining Pleasure, Serves Two . . . .

When Served to Four or More, Add a Liter of Wine - Our Compliments

Crab Cocktail . . . .

Shrimp Cocktail . . . .

Small Appetite Menu

Served with Soup or Salad, Fries or Baked Potato or Rice, Vegetable and Coffee, Tea or Sanka

SCALLOPS
JUMBO PRAWNS
GROUND BEEF STEAK
FRIED CHICKEN
PACIFIC OYSTERS
FISH AND CHIPS
STEAMER CLAMS

Please Note: Much of Our Seafood is Seasonal, Ask Your Waitress if it is Available - Thank You

Junior Orders

Hamburger . . . .
Cheeseburger . . . .
Crab Sandwich . . . .
with Melted Cheese . . . .
Clam Sandwich . . . .

Side Orders

Mushrooms Cooked in Butter . . . .
Asparagus, Buttered . . . .
French Fries . . . .
Baked Potato . . . .
Vegetable of the Day . . . .

Beverages

Coffee . . . .
Tea . . . .
Soft Drinks . . . .
Wine, Glass . . . .
Sanka . . . .
Milk . . . .
Iced Tea . . . .

Dessert

The Feed Store Special Dessert is a Blintz Filled with Sour Cream or Whipped Topping and Your Choice of Strawberry or Orange Sauce

One - ____ Two - ______

Western food is blend of colors, flavors and textures with a rich heritage of style and taste. Spices and herbs are treated with respect. Freshness and naturalness are revered. Variety is a must.

Dinner Entrees

Country Specials

PRIME RIB OF BEEF au Jus,
Full Cut, 12 oz. . . . .
Small Cut, 8 oz. . . . .
with Creamed Horseradish

GROUND BEEF STEAK . . . .
with Mushrooms

CHICKEN KIEV . . . .
Breast of Chicken, Butter and Herbs

NEW YORK CUT STEAK, 12 oz. . . .

RIB EYE STEAK, 12 oz. . . . .

TOP SIRLOIN STEAK,
Full Cut, 12 oz. . . . .
Small Cut, 8 oz. . . . .

VEAL HONGORISE . . . .
with Sour Cream Sauce

Seafood Fare

CRAB LEGS, Deep Fried to a Golden Brown or Sauteed . . . .

RAZOR CLAMS, From Our Local Beaches . . . .

JUMBO PRAWNS, Lightly Breaded for True Flavor . . . .

SEA SCALLOPS, Deep Fried to a Golden Brown or Sauteed . . . .

SALMON STEAK, Columbia River Fish . . . .

HALIBUT STEAK, Almondine Style . . . .

LOBSTER TAIL, Australian, One . . . . ____ Two . . . . ____

CRAB CASSEROLE, a Bubbling Casserole in a Rich Cheese Sauce . . . .

CAPTAIN'S PLATTER, an Assortment of Deep Fried Fish, Oysters, Clams and Prawns . . . .

CRAB PICNIC, Dungeness Crab, Served Cold with a Barbecue and Vermouth Sauce for Dipping . . . .

KING NEPTUNE CASSEROLE, Shrimp, Scallops, Crab and Cod in Our Excellent Sauce . . . .

OYSTERS, Deep Fried . . . .

FISH AND CHIPS, Deep Fried White Fish . . . .

Above Dinners Served with Salad and Choice of Potato or Rice Pilaf, Bread and Coffee, Tea or Sanka

Our Sweetheart Combinations

JUMBO PRAWNS & STEAK . . . .

LOBSTER TAIL & STEAK . . . .

PACIFIC OYSTERS & STEAK . . . .

SEASIDE RAZOR CLAMS & STEAK . . . .

LANGOSTINO & STEAK . . . .

Above Dinners Served with Rib Eye Steak and Your Choice of Seafood Entree, Salad, Choice of Potato or Rice Pilaf, Bread, and Coffee, Tea or Sanka

FULL DINNER SERVICE AFTER 5:00 P.M.

To some it's an Irish Pub; others call it a family pub. Regardless of what you call it, Fiddlers Green is another way of capturing old world charm. The massive wooden bar, which has been serving customers since Prohibition ended, and the wood stove help set the ambience. Owner Terri Maddox has even included a piano and a gut bucket (a stringed instrument) to gather around for the sing-alongs. All in all, it's a warm and friendly place where the common denominator is fun. Whatever your state of mind when you enter, we're convinced Fiddlers Green will put a smile on your face.

Fiddlers Green
218 West Marine Drive
Astoria, OR 97103

325-4802

Hours: 10 am-10 pm Tues.-Thurs.
10 am-1 am Fri.-Sat.
Food served 11 am-10 pm
Closed all major holidays

Libations: Wine and beer

Payment: VISA and
Mastercharge

Reservations: Suggested for
summer

Fiddlers Green

Chocolate Mousse

4 ounces semi-sweet chocolate
1 ounce unsweetened chocolate
4 tablespoons butter
3 egg yolks
6 egg whites
1 tablespoon sugar
⅛ teaspoon almond extract
1 cup heavy cream
juice of ½ lemon
almonds (optional)
chocolate curls (optional)

Melt chocolate in double boiler. Add butter, one tablespoon at a time. Cool well in refrigerator while separating eggs. Whip cream. Beat egg whites until stiff. Add sugar and almond extract to egg whites. Remove chocolate mixture from refrigerator and stir in lemon juice. Then add egg yolks, one at a time. Fold in whipped cream and then egg whites into chocolate mixture. Pour into champagne glasses and chill. Just before serving, garnish with whipped cream and almonds or chocolate curls if desired. Serves 6.

Entrees

dinners at Fiddler's are accompanied by french onion soup, salad, choice of stuffed potatoe or rice pilaf, fresh vegtables, and a bran muffin.

~ cioppino ~

~ a delightful stew of prawns, crab, and steamer clams simmered in their shells with whitefish in a rich tomatoe wine sauce.

~ shrimp malcomb ~

~ deep fried in a beer batter specially seasoned with ginger and tarragon.

~ captain's platter ~

~ a variety of deep-fried prawns, scallops, oysters, and whitefish.

~ brochette of beef flambé ~

~ marinated chunks of beef tenderloin and vegetables, skewered, broiled and flamed at your table.

~ Fiddler's Special Steak ~

~ a choice 8 oz. New York cut

~ steak and prawns or oysters ~

~ your choice with an 8 oz. New York

~ chicken almond crisp ~

~ one-half chicken poached in wine and almonds, dredged in a seasoned coating and fried.

~ chicken cordon bleu ~

~ tender breast of chicken stuffed with swiss cheese and ham.

~ catch of the day ~

~ fresh seafood of the season.

~ prime rib ~

~ available on Friday and Saturday

Lighter Fare

-fish and chips-
~ tender whitefish and homemade fries served with a tossed salad.

-pot of stew-
~ Fiddler's own and Irish too! served with a tossed salad and onion roll.

-hamburger-
~ served atop an onion roll with homemade fries and a tossed salad.

-Quiche-
~ a speciality prepared daily, served with a tossed salad and a bran muffin.

-Appetizers and Accompaniments-

. . .

-seafood hors d'oeuvres platter-
~ a rich assortment of delicacies from the sea.

-Fiddler's french onion soup-
~ liberally topped with parmesan cheese.

-tossed green salad-
~ fresh greens, beets, tomatoes and a warm french roll.

-stuffed baked potatoe-
~ a classic! stuffed with sour cream, chives, butter and bacon.

-basket of onion rings-
~ crisp and golden fried

-basket of homemade fries-
~ fresh and home-fried, an almost forgotten pleasure!

- assorted desserts-

Hara's Dining Room

HARA'S Dining Room carries on a long tradition of refined elegance in the northern coastal region. It's one of those places reserved for a special time. One of the more formal restaurants, Hara's strives for the memorable, transforming an ordinary evening into an event. White linen tablecloths and napkins contrast the conspicuously central open fireplace, which bestows warmth and congeniality to the surroundings. Owner Bob Girtle has a personal commitment to having his dining room please both the eye and the palate and graciously insists on the smooth, unhurried service which characterizes Hara's. Here is an opportunity for distinctive continental dining.

Hara's Dining Room
227 Broadway
P.O. Box 325
Seaside, OR 97138

738-6701

Hours: Summer 5 pm-11 pm daily
Winter 5 pm-11 pm Wed.-Sun.
Lounge open until 2:30

Libations: Full wine list, cocktails, and beer

Payment: VISA, Mastercharge,
American Express, personal checks

Reservations: Encouraged

Hara's Beef Stroganoff

1 pound beef sirloin steak, cut into thin strips
1 tablespoon flour
½ teaspoon salt
2 tablespoons butter
sliced fresh mushrooms
½ cup chopped onion
1 clove garlic, peeled and pressed
2 tablespoons butter
3 tablespoons flour
1 tablespoon tomato paste
2 cups condensed beef broth
dry white wine to suit

Coat beef strips with mixture of flour and salt. Brown in butter. Add mushrooms, onion and garlic. Cook until tender, 3-4 minutes. Remove meat and mushrooms from pan. Add butter to pan drippings and blend in flour. Add tomato paste and stir in broth. Cook and stir over medium heat until thickened and bubbly. Return meat and mushrooms to skillet. Stir in sour cream and white wine. Cook slowly until heated through. Serve over buttered egg noodles. Serves 4.

INCLUDED WITH YOUR DINNERS
Choice of Tossed Green Salad or
Boston Baby Clam Soup
Baked Potatoe, Au Gratin, Rice Pilaff or Egg Noodles Parmesan

Boeuf

Hara's Stroganof of Boeuf
With buttered egg noodles parmesan - the house speciality.

Hara's Peppercorn Steak
'Prime Cut of Net York Steak'
Seasoned with freshly cracked peppercorns to preserve natural juices.

Chopped Sirloin of Boeuf
Mushrooms sautted in sherry

Top Sirloin Thick and Juicy — The Tastiest of the Steaks
small
large

New York Steak
Prime Kansas Corn Fed Beef

Petite Filet'
Not too much, not too little.

Boeuf Kabab Flambe'
Served flaming on a bed of rice.

Filet Mignon
Aged & pampered

Chateaubriand Diablo
per person
Recognized the world over as a gourmet's choice. Garnished with baby vegetables et mushrooms. Served flaming for two or more.

Lobster et Steak
A delightful marriage.

Combination Top Sirloin and Jumbo Prawns

Hara's Peppered Rib Eye
'Eye of the Prime Rib'
Marinated for days in a concoction of Hara's saucy chef seasoning, olive oil, wine. Roasted for two hours over a very slow fire.

King Cut
Queen Cut

Cornish Game Hen
Stuffed with Apple-Walnut Dressing and Garnished with Broiled Tomato

We can not guarantee steaks well done.

Poissons

Crab Frederick
Prepared with fresh shallots and mushrooms. Served with Rice Pilaff en Casserole.

Seafood Omelet
Crab, Shrimp, Mushrooms & Green Pepper.

Petrole Sole
Stuffed with Crab & Shrimp Oved baked in white wine sauce

Les Petites Oysters
A gourmet delicacy. Saute'd or deep fried.

Baby Scallops
Saute'd to perfection. Served with egg noodles parmesan and vegetable dish. Deep fried, if you desire.

Steamed Little Neck Clams
With nectar et drawn butter

The Crab's Thighs
Saute'd in wine and butter or lightly breaded and deep fried.

French Fried Jumbo Prawns
— or Saute'd

Neptune's Platter
A lovely array of petite oysters, crab thighs, scallops et prawns.

Also with Lobster

Seafood Marguray
A delightful blending of chicken breast, scallops, prawns, little neck clams and tastefully saute'd in wine

Baked Pacific Salmon Filet
Very delicately baked in lemon butter to preserve the natural juices. (when available)

Dungeness Crab Newberg
Fresh mushrooms, wine sauce, golden glazed and sprinkled with parmesan.

Broiled Lobster Tail
Cooked to perfection in a sherried butter sauce served with drawn butter

CRAB BROILER

One of America's Outstanding
Roadside Restaurants

THE Crab Broiler may have begun as a roadside cafe, but today it is a polished restaurant acclaimed as one of America's outstanding dining establishments, having been featured by numerous publications including Ford Times and Life Magazine. The sparkling decor is highlighted by stained glass windows, hanging foliage, antiques, 3 brick fireplaces and the beauty of 11 different woods. There's a well-stocked gift shop adjacent to the entrance, and a Japanese garden circles the building. The dedicated and personal involvement that comes from 32 years of Daggatt family ownership is evident everywhere, but its continuing popularity with travellers is the Crab Broiler's best recommendation.

Crab Broiler
Box 315, Hamlet Route
Junction of Highway 101 &
3 miles south of Seaside
Seaside, OR 97138

738-5313

Hours: Summer 11:30 am-10 pm daily
Winter 11:30 am-9 pm daily
Closed Thanksgiving and Christmas

Libations: Full wine list, cocktails, and beer

Payment: Cash only

Reservations: Suggested

Crab Broiler

Barbecued Crab

Dungeness crab (one per person), cooked, cleaned, cracked

1 quart fancy catsup
10 whole cloves
1 teaspoon horseradish
2 tablespoons Worcestershire sauce
1 teaspoon thyme
2 teaspoons all seasoning salt
1 teaspoon MSG
4 bay leaves
1 teaspoon sugar
½ teaspoon salt

Mix all ingredients together and add enough water to make a light sauce. Heat to boiling point. May be used hot or cold as a cocktail sauce. We suggest this same sauce may be combined with crabmeat and served hot as an open-faced crab sandwich.

Take one Dungeness crab per person and place in ½ gallon of near-boiling water that is seasoned with bay leaves and cloves. As soon as crabmeat is warmed throughout, drain. Put crab in barbecue sauce and let sit for ten minutes.

Place crab on serving plate and use remaining sauce in bowl for dunking. Serving suggestions: white wine, garlic bread, finger bowl and plenty of napkins. We supply a bib to each customer.

Sandwiches

CRAB, PLAIN. . . . with Old English melted cheese. . . . .
CRAB, BAR-B-Q . . with Old English melted cheese. . . . .
CLAMS — 2 Clams, served open faced . . . .
OYSTERS — 3 Oysters, served open faced . . . .
CHEESEBURGER — Ground steer beef . . . .
HAMBURGER — Ground steer beef . . . .
TUNA FISH. . . . . . with melted cheese . . . .

Side Orders

FRENCH FRIES . . . .
SIDE OF VEGETABLES. . . . .
ONION RINGS . . . .
GARLIC BREAD, made with fresh garlic . . . .
SIDE OF COLE SLAW (or tossed green salad). . . . .
SIDE OF BARBECUE SAUCE (our own) . . . .
BLEU CHEESE BREAD, better try some . . . .
BAKED POTATO . . . .

Appetizers

PETITE OYSTER COCKTAIL — Served with Red Sauce, lemon and crackers . . . .
SHRIMP COCKTAIL — Served with lemon and cracker. Red Sauce or 1000 Dressing . . . .
CRAB LEG COCKTAIL — Served with lemon and crackers. Red Sauce or 1000 Island Dressing. . . . .
CRAB COCKTAIL — Served with lemon and cracker. Red Sauce or 1000 Island Dressing . . . .
TOMATO, GRAPEFRUIT OR PINEAPPLE JUICE. . . . .

Soups

CLAM CHOWDER — Homemade (Boston style with milk) Large bowl . . . . Small Bowl . .
OYSTER STEW — Pacific oysters, made with milk and butter . . . .
PETITE OYSTER STEW . . . . If you prefer made with cream . . . .
CANNED SOUPS — Heinz or Campbell's . . . .

Salads

CRAB LOUIS a la Crab Broiler — with our Special 1000 Island Dressing and choice of bread . . . . Large . . . . Small
SHRIMP LOUIS a la Crab Broiler — with our own Special 1000 Island Dressing and choice of bread. . . . . Large . . . . Small
PINEAPPLE AND COTTAGE CHEESE. . . . . Large . . . . Small
FRUIT SALAD — Choice of dressing and bread . . . . Large . . . . Small

Desserts

PIE AND CAKE — (From our own bakery — Choose from the pastry tray which your waitress will bring for **your** selection . . . . A LA MODE . . . .
ICE CREAM. . . . .
CHOCOLATE SUNDAE . . . .

Beverages

HOT CHOCOLATE . . . .
ICED TEA. . . . .
ICED COFFEE . . . .
COFFEE . . . .
TEA. . . . .
MILK . . . .
SANKA (pot). . . . .
SKIM MILK . . . .
CHOCOLATE MILK . . . .
SOFT DRINKS . . . .

Dinner Entrees

Dinner items listed below are served with Garlic, Plain or Bleu Cheese Bread, Potatoes, Cole Slaw or Tossed Green Salad and Coffee, Tea or Sanka
extra for service plate

Chicken

CHICKEN — Ranch Fresh — one of our most popular dishes (Please allow 20 minutes). . . . .

From the Broiler

Steaks and Chops

(All weights are uncooked weights)

STEAK SANDWICH — 6 oz. Steak, Served on Toast . . . .
TENDERLOIN STEAK — (Broiled Choice Aged Beef) . . . .
NEW YORK STEAK — (Broiled Choice Aged Beef) . . . . 8 oz. . . . 12 oz. . .
RIB EYE STEAK — (Broiled Choice Aged Beef) . . . . 8 oz. . . . 12 oz. . .
"T" BONE STEAK — 16 oz. Delicious . . . .
HAMBURGER STEAK — (Ground Choice Steer Beef with onions). . . . .
SALISBURY STEAK — Topped with Mushroom Sauce . . . .
PORK CHOPS — (Please allow 15 minutes for Pork Chops) . . . .
STEAK & LOBSTER . . . .
LOBSTER TAIL. . . . . One . . . Two .

We cannot guarantee tenderness of steaks ordered well done.

HAM OR BACON & LARGE GRADE AA EGGS — Served with Toast, Jelly, Potatoes and Coffee or Tea . . . .

Ocean Seafood

CRAB AU GRATIN — A bubbling casserole of Crab meat blended in a rich cheese sauce . . . .
BARBECUE CRAB — (Shell Crab served with our special hot Barbecue sauce served over the crab and with extra bowl of sauce) You pick the meat from the shell and wear a bib when eating it — delicious . . . .
CRACKED CRAB — You pick the white, firm, delicious meat from the shell — A "Gourmet's Delight" Served cold with drawn butter or mayonnaise . . . .
FILET OF SOLE — Served with lemon and Tartar Sauce . . . .
PETITE OYSTERS — For a Gourmet Delight have these tender delightful morsels of goodness, lightly fried. . . . .
SEASIDE RAZOR CLAMS — Dug on our own local beach . . . .
FISH AND CHIPS — Deep fried white fish — Tartar Sauce. . . . .
HALIBUT STEAK — Served with lemon and Tartar Sauce . . . .
DUNGENESS CRAB LEGS — Whole Crab Legs — deep fried to a golden brown . . . .
We consider this the most delectable way of serving crab — Choice of Cocktail or Tartar Sauce
DEEP SEA SCALLOPS — Served with Tartar Sauce. . . . .
FRIED SHRIMP — Served with our own Shrimp Sauce . . . .
BROILED SALMON — Caught locally. Lemon Butter — Perfection (When in Season). . . . .
STEAMED CLAMS — Served with drawn butter. . . . .
_ MBINATION SEAFOOD PLATE — Clam, Scallops, Shrimp, Oysters, White Fish, Crab Legs . . . .
F.ED OYSTERS — (Oysters deep fried to a golden brown) — Tartar Sauce. . . . .

THE WHALER

THE Whaler is a nautical showplace; it fairly sings of salt air and sea voyages. Hatch covers have been transformed into table tops; ship's doors form the front doors; and the walls hold an assortment of wheels, portholes, charts and hangings. But there is more here than pleasant surroundings. The imaginative and extensive menu is frequently enhanced by nightly specials. "Early Bird" and "Senior Citizen" discounts are offered regularly as well. Owner David Firebaugh built The Whaler almost twenty years ago, and, with daughter and son-in-law Sandra and Doug Larson, has guided its development into one of the North Coast's very best.

The Whaler
Corner of 2nd & Hemlock
P.O. Box 455
Cannon Beach, OR 97110

436-2821

Hours: Summer 4-11 pm weekdays
4 pm-midnight and weekends
Winter 4-10 pm weekdays
4-11 pm weekends
Closed Wed. and Thurs. year-round and
from Jan. 1 to Feb. 14

Libations: Full wine list, cocktails, and beer

Payment: VISA, and Mastercharge

Reservations: Suggested for large groups

The Whaler

Peanut Butter Pie

1 cup peanut butter
1 cup sugar
8 ounces cream cheese
2 tablespoons melted butter
1 pint heavy cream
1 tablespoon vanilla extract
1 baked pie shell
fudge topping

Cream the peanut butter, sugar, cream cheese, and butter together. Whip cream and vanilla. Mix it all together and pour into baked pie shell. Dribble fudge topping over the top. Serves 6-8.

Thar She Blows

A sighting has been made. You're off to a good start. Our lookout hasn't spotted a pod of whales but he has located a whole passel of rare and unique appetizers and cocktails that are worth "heading into."

Cocktails

Served with Devil's red sauce — it's hot!

CRAB COCKTAIL . . . .

SHRIMP COCKTAIL . . . . . .

EXTRA-SMALL OYSTERS . . . .

MARINATED FISH COCKTAIL . . . .

Appetizers

SHRIMP SESAME . . . .
SAUTEED CRAB LEGS LAROUSSE . . . .
ICED PRAWNS . . . .
TERIYAKI BEEF . . . .
MARINATED FISH . . . .
WHALER'S TRAY . . . .
Serves Two or More. Combination of above hors d'oeuvres
SCAMPI . . . .
STEAMED CLAMS . . . .

All above served with garlic bread.

Where Away?

The call for directions so you'll know which way to head. You can't go wrong if you head for the soup.

GALLEY SOUP . . . .
Changes with the cook's whim and the ship's stores.

CALM CLAM CHOWDER . . .
Too heavy with clams to make waves.

TURN-TO OYSTER STEW . .
If this oyster stew doesn't get you headed in the right direction, nothing will.

Greenie's

If it's your first day on a Whaler, you're a Greenie, but we promise you'll not be any greener than this collection of cool, crisp green salads. By the way, all of the dressings are in our own galley. Take o'pint home.

CAPTAIN'S LOUIS . . . .
Choice of fresh crab or shrimp or both heaped on. A Captain's size portion.

MATE'S LOUIS . . . .
Choice of fresh crab or shrimp or both heaped on. A Mate's size portion.

GALLEY SALAD . . . .
It's an assortment - don't ask of what. We guarantee everything that's in it is legal - and delicious.

LARGE TOSS . . . .
Cool, crisp mixed greens with choice of dressing.

Sperm Whale's Preference

The sperm whale was the most hunted whale because he would yield the most oil and whalebone. He was also one of the most dangerous whales because he himself is a hunter. With his 25-foot jaw lined with razor edge teeth he was capable of stoving in a boat with all the men in it. However, rather than whaleboats his preference would lean to any one of the seafoods presented here for your dining enjoyment. (Bet you didn't know you had so much in common with a whale.) Actually, you get the best deal because all the whale would get is the seafood.

You get the seafood of your choice and relish dish, Galley soup, tossed salad, choice of rice, rice pilaf, French fried, baked or au gratin potato, and Whaler's bread – garlic or cheese.

Sea Legs For The Landlubber

If you're a little unsteady at sea and prefer to keep one foot on the shore - here are the perfect entrees.
Served with the complete dinner.

WHALER RAZOR CLAMS ....
Freshly dug from just up the beach a piece

EXTRA-SMALL OYSTERS ....
Tenderly sauteed

STEAMED LITTLE-NECK CLAMS................
Served in sand bucket with drawn butter.

SCAMPI SAUTE ....
Succulent scampi, beautifully sauteed and served in their shells with our specially seasoned butter - a delight for any landlubber or sailor

COLUMBIA RIVER SALMON ....
Served with dill butter

FILET MIGNON & LOBSTER ....

LOBSTER TAIL, 10 oz.....

OCEAN-FRESH HALIBUT . .
Served with dill butter

CRAB LEGS – Sauteed a la Larousse ....
Larousse was a fancy French chef who really had a way with crab legs!

CAP'N 'n CREW ....
A collection of seafood — shrimp, scallops, oysters, razor clam, white fish — no blubber in sight!

DEEP-SEA SCALLOPS ....
Flowers of the deep, deep-fried or sauteed in dill butter

PRAWNS ....
What's your pleasure? Deep-fried or sauteed in dill butter

PACIFIC WHITE FISH ......
Beautifully fried to a golden-brown

FILET MIGNON & SCAMPI ....

CHEF'S SPECIAL OF THE DAY ....

These complete dinners include "specially selected" Wine for Two.

"Wood to Black Skin"

With a whale all picked out, the harpooner poised for the strike, would call to the men to row "wood to black skin," until the boat was against the side of the whale.

You'll want to get as close to one of these U.S.D.A. choice steaks as possible. Make your selection, stand poised, ready to sink the "harpoon" and we'll see that you get into position to make a strike.

When you connect you will be making a "whale of a deal" because your choice steak is broiled to taste and served with relish dish, Galley soup, Greenie salad, choice of rice, rice pilaf, French fries, baked or au gratin potato, and Whaler's bread - garlic or cheese.

NEW YORK STEAK—12 oz. *Cut for dimension* . . . .

FILET MIGNON—10 oz. *Tenderest steak on the steer* . . .

CAPTAIN'S SIZE TOP SIRLOIN – 12 oz. *Flavor with heft*

FIRST MATE SIZE – 8 oz. *Full flavor on a smaller scale*

BOS'N SIZE – 6 oz. *Every bit as good as the Captain's* . .

PRIME GROUND STEAK – 10 oz. . . . .

MARINATED PEPPER STEAK *—Exotically different* . .

LAMB GOURMET

Delectable lamb shank cooked to perfection and served with a sour cream sauce laced with herbs on a bed of rice.

Lobcouse for Two

(Bouillabaisse)

CRAB COOKING OLYMPICS AWARD WINNER

A unique conçoction of white fish, salmon, shell fish, and Dungeness crab simmered in fine seafood stock and served in a tureen.

The Lobcouse Dinner includes "Specially Selected" Wine for Two

Rack of Lamb For Two

Baked to perfection, surrounded with an array of garden vegetables and our own hot mint sauce.

or

Double Cut New York Steak for Two

Two pounds of choice New York Cut steer beef broiled to taste and served on a plank.

These complete dinners include "Specially Selected" Wine for Two

Fancy Favorites

A whaler might never put to sea if he knew
he could get these fancy favorites on shore.

Each complete with relish tray,
Galley soup, tossed salad, rice, vegetable, and
Whaler's bread – garlic or cheese.

CRAB RAREBIT . . . .
Served on a delicate bed of rice, with our own cheese sauce.

SHRIMP RAREBIT . . . .
Served on a delicate bed of rice, with our own cheese sauce.

CHICKEN KIEV . . . .
Breast of chicken stuffed with spiced butter and wine.

CHICKEN . . . .
Half a chicken, deep fried for even flavor – moist and tender.

Whaler Sandwiches

To a whaleman they are a snack, to anyone else they are a meal!

Each is served with dinner salad and French fries.

CHOICE BEEF STEAK SANDWICH
8 oz. . . . . **6 oz.** . . . .

OPEN FACE GROUND BEEF-8 oz.
On French bread . . . .

FRENCH DIP - au jus . . . .

CRAB SANDWICH - ***With chef Steven's own special sauce topped with aged Tillamook Cheddar*** . . . .

Young Pikes

(For guests as old as 12 or as young as 70)

Your choice -

FRIED CHICKEN • GROUND BEEF
WHITE FISH • SALMON • PRAWNS • STEAK

Each is served with salad, French fries and ice cream.

HAYSTACK House is warm and tastefully appointed. The walls are shingled and form a pleasant backdrop for the many sculptures, carvings and paintings. The abundant use of stained glass colors the wood and adds to the elegant yet casual feeling created by the central fireplace. The intimacy that owner Margaret Casey has brought to the Haystack House softens the harshness of the surf, roaring just outside. Her guests can watch driftwood and an occasional glass float being cast upon the beach as they dine on the tempting fare of Randy Watts, who is determined that the quality of food must at least equal that of the view.

Haystack House at Tolovana Inn
Highway 101, Beach Loop, south of
Cannon Beach
P.O. Box 345
Cannon Beach, OR 97145

436-1111

Hours: Summer 9 am-11 pm daily except Sun.
Winter 11 am-9 pm weekdays
9 am-10 pm Sat.
Sun. year-round 9 am-9 pm
Closed Christmas Day

Libations: Full wine list, cocktails, and beer

Payment: VISA and Mastercharge
No personal checks

Reservations: Not accepted

Haystack House Lobster Thermidor

1 lobster (11 ounces approximately)
2 cups Mornay sauce
1 hard boiled egg, grated
6 whole olives, halved
1 shot Triple Sec Orange Liqueur or Grand Marnier
¼ teaspoon cayenne pepper
1 teaspoon lemon juice

Remove lobster from shell and cut into 8 pieces, reserving the shell. Saute lobster pieces in olive oil until firm. Blend together the Mornay sauce, cayenne pepper and Triple Sec in bowl.

Place lobster shell in ramkin. Add a layer of sauce in bottom of shell, add lobster pieces and cover with remaining sauce. Sprinkle top with grated egg and olives. Bake 8-10 minutes at 350°F. Serves 1.

Appetizers

ESCARGOT A LA BOURGUIGNONNE..

CRAB COCKTAIL....................................

OYSTER COCKTAIL................................

SHRIMP COCKTAIL................................

ONION RINGS....................................

STEAMED BUTTER CLAMS.........

APPETIZER PLATE...........................

MUSHROOMS sautéed in butter, burgundy and garlic..........................

Soups

CLAM CHOWDER....................................

SOUP OF THE DAY................................

Salads

CRAB LOUIS...

SHRIMP LOUIS...................................

TOSSED GREEN SALAD..................

SALAD BAR ....

Side Orders

MUSHROOMS....................................
sautéed in butter burgundy and garlic

RICE PILAF...

ONION RINGS....................................

VEGETABLE OF THE DAY.............

FRENCH FRIES ....

BAKED POTATO ....

Beverages

COFFEE ....

TEA ....

MILK ....

SOFT DRINKS ....

Desserts

ICE CREAM ....

SHERBET ....

CHERRIES JUBILEE FOR TWO.....

CHEESE CAKE ....

Junior Portions

Under 12 years of age

CHOICE OF: Sole - Deep Fried Scallops - Deep Fried Prawns - Hamburger Steak with Tossed Salad and French Fries

NO CHECKS CASHED — NO SUBSTITUTIONS - NO RESERVATIONS
MINIMUM CHARGE — PER PERSON

Haystack House Specialties

All dinners include, except where specified, soup or salad bar, choice of baked potato, rice pilaf, French fries or vegetable of the day, and fresh baked bread.

TERIYAKI STEAK - served in delightful Hawaiian style with rice pilaf..........................

PEPPERCORN- specially selected New York, smothered in fresh, cracked peppercorns, broiled to your taste..........................

CRAB CASSEROLE - fresh crab (in season) smothered in a tangy Mornay sauce..............

OYSTERS FLORENTINE- baked on a bed of rock salt, topped with a dash of spinach, hard cooked egg and Mornay sauce..........................

SAUTÉED CRAB LEGS - a gourmet delight. Crab legs sautéed in butter and sherry with green onions and fresh mushrooms ....

LOBSTER - one of the sea's great treasures; broiled and served with drawn butter...........

LOBSTER THERMIDOR — A gourmet delight you will never forget. Tender lobster sautéed in butter, in a casserole with Sauterne Mornay sauce..........................

From the Sea

SALMON - fresh Columbia River Chinook. Served only in season..............................Seasonal

PRAWNS - scampi style basted in butter and herbs, laced in Chablis..........................

STEAMED CLAMS - a miniature delicacy served with drawn butter and lemon wedges......

RAZOR CLAMS - tender and tasty. A specialty from our own beautiful sandy beaches........

SCALLOPS - Alaskan scallops sautéed in butter, herbs, and wine. Served with rice pilaf......

FILET OF HALIBUT - from the icy waters of the Northern Sea, tender and flaky.............

GRILLED FRESH SMALL OYSTERS - gently grilled, served with tartar sauce.................

CAPTAIN'S CHOICE - combination of fresh small oysters, scallops, prawns, crab legs and razor clam..........................

FILET of SOLE ALMONDINE - choice sole, grilled to perfection with sliced almonds......

STEAK & SEAFOOD - where the Sea meets the Shore. Your choice of lobster tail or scampi style Prawn with a 6 oz. steak..........................

From the Broiler

TOP SIRLOIN - thick and juicy, most flavorful of the steaks.......... small ....large

FILET MIGNON - King of the red meats..........................

NEW YORK - the succulent steak that is a favorite by the sea..........................

BEEF KEBAB - tender pieces of beef intermingled with green peppers, onions, tomatoes, button mushrooms, served on a bed of rice pilaf..........................

STEAK SANDWICH - Haystack House favorite steak sandwich served on garlic bread with tossed salad and French fries..........................

Manzanita Inn

CHISELED out of heavily timbered lands sloping into the sea, Manzanita is a bit off the beaten path of Highway 101. Right in the heart of town is the Manzanita Inn, a uniquely coastal dining establishment with an atmosphere all its own. Owner Ted Pankowski's founding philosophy was "If I cooked what I like, maybe others would like it too". Time has proven they do, indeed; the Inn is consistently busy with a colorful mix of locals and tourists. The format is informal and fun, with centrally located open kitchen and blackboard menu reflecting current availability. Ted likes to call it an "alternative" restaurant; we think you'll find it a very special place as well.

Manzanita Inn
165 Laneda
(1-½ blocks from ocean)
Manzanita, OR 97130

368-6189

Hours: March-October 5 pm-10 pm daily
November-February 5 pm-10 pm
Thurs.-Sun.
11 am-3 pm Sat.-Sun. lunch/brunch

Libations: Selected wine list, cocktails, and beer

Payment: VISA, Mastercharge, checks

Reservations: Telephone for current hours and reservations

Manzanita Inn

Oysters Kilpatrick

Sauté fresh oysters (drained) in butter, lemon juice, and any respectable dry white wine.

Add fresh mushrooms (sliced), chopped green onions or chives, and a pinch of dill.

When cooked through (this should have a gentle touch), add crumbled bits of crisp bacon.

Top with a splash of Worcestershire sauce and sprinkles of parsley. Serve hot in a shell or shallow dish.

Manzanita Inn

Dinners include soup, salad,
homemade "Inn" bread
and fresh vegetables

- Steamed Clams
- Geoduck Clam Steak
- Scallops St. Jacques
- 8 oz. Filet Mignon
- Scallops St. Jacques
- 8 oz. Filet Mignon
  (with Sauteed Scampi)
- Sauteed Scampi
- Oysters Kilpatrick
- Crab & Clam Cioppino
- Breast of Chicken Supreme
- Filet of Sole with Shrimp
- Clam & Shrimp Chowder
- Spiced Ham Steak
- Chinook / Silver Salmon (varies on season)
- Prime Rib (Sundays only)
- Cracked Dungeness Crab (varies on season)
- Razor Clams (grilled) (varies on season)

Senior Citizens' Discounts and Children's Portions

River Sea Inn

THE River Sea Inn, nestled in the little town of Wheeler, fits quietly into the landscape. The view from the informal dining area is alive with a sweeping panorama of Nehalem River and Bay. Neahkahnie Mountain, where legend says a pirate treasure is buried, stands in the background. Owner Nick Recio brought with him 30 years of experience in the restaurant business. A member of the Chef de Quisine Society, Nick runs the kitchen with the skilled hand you would expect given his background; the food is consistently first rate.

River Sea Inn
380 Marine Drive
P.O. Box 51
Wheeler, OR 97147

368-5789

Hours: Summer 11:30 am-10 pm weekdays,
11 pm Fri.-Sat.
Winter 11:30 am- 9 pm weekdays,
10 pm Fri.-Sat.
Open 10 am on Sundays
Closed Mondays in Winter, and all major holidays

Libations: Beer and wine

Payment: VISA, Mastercharge, checks

Reservations: Suggested for large parties

River Sea Inn

Flan

(an authentic Spanish dessert)

Caramel Topping

Place in a saucepan 2 tablespoons water and ¼ cup sugar. Stir constantly over medium heat until it liquefies and turns golden brown. Place 1 teaspoon into lightly buttered cups and set aside.

Custard

Break into blender 4 eggs; whip until lemon colored. Add ¼ teaspoon vanilla extract and 2½ cups milk; mix. Fill custard cups and sprinkle with nutmeg. Set cups into a pan; put pan into oven; pour water around cups until ¾ from top. Bake for 1 hour at 300°F.; test with toothpick. Remove and cool, then chill in refrigerator. Slide knife around inside of cup to loosen custard and carefully turn upside down into dish; top with whipped cream. Serves 4.

River Sea Inn
DINNER MENU

Appetizer

Local Bay Shrimp Cocktail Supreme. . . . .

Local Fresh Oyster Cocktail Supreme. . . . .

Guacamole Supreme . . . served with Corn Chips . . . .

Salad

Bay Shrimp Louis . . . Served with Soup Du Jour . . . .
Local Bay Shrimp nested on a bed of Greens with Louis Dressing and Garnish, Roll and Butter

House Specialty . . . Mexican Food

Served with Soup or Salad . . . Choice of Dressing . . . Corn Chips and Hot Sauce

#1 Uno Choice of One. . . . .
Beef Taco, Beef Enchilada, Cheese Enchilada or Chili Relleno served with Refried Beans and Spanish Rice

#2 Dos Choice of Two . . . .
Beef Taco, Beef Enchilada, Cheese Enchilada or Chili Relleno served with Refried Beans and Spanish Rice

#3 Tres Tostada de la Casa . . . .
Crisp Corn Tortilla topped with Refried Beans, Beef, Cheese, Mixed Greens, Tomato and Avocado

#4 Quatro Burrito . . . .
A large Flour Tortilla filled with Beef, Cheese, Onions and Refried Beans topped with Ranchera Sauce and Melted Cheese served with Spanish Rice

Chef Recommends

Boneless Breast of Chicken Bordelaise . . . .
Sauteed in Butter . . . Garnished with Mushroom Wine Sauce

Veal Provencale. . . . .
Tender Milk Fed Veal Sauteed in Butter . . . topped with Avocado, Tomato and Mornev Glace

Steak Neptune . . . .
Choice Sirloin topped with Bay Shrimp and Wine Sauce

From The Lakes And Seas

With your Dinner we serve a fresh Mixed Green Salad with our Homemade Dressings of Blue Cheese, Thousand Island and Tarragon French Dressing or Soup Du Jour. Spanish Rice or Baked Potato, Oven Fresh Rolls and Butter.

Catch of The Day . . . Ling Cod or Red Snapper . . . Lemon Butter . . . .
Local Ocean Fish Cooked to Perfection

Deep Fried Oysters . . . with Tartar Sauce . . . .
Local Oysters Delicately Fried Golden Brown

Mixed Seafood Grill . . . with Tartar Sauce . . . .
A combination of delicious Filet of Sole, Shrimp and Tender Scallops, Oysters and Fish, delicately Deep Fried.

Mahi Mahi Tropicana . . . Sauteed in Butter and Lemon Juice . . . .
Topped with Fresh Pineapple, Coconut and Almonds

Boneless Sauteed Trout Almondine . . . .
Topped with Almonds, Sauteed in Lemon Butter

From The Broiler

Choice Sirloin Steak . . . Maitre De Butter . . . .
A Thick Cut of Choice Sirloin, Broiled to Perfection

Brochette of Beef . . . .
Tender Chunks of Sirloin on a Skewer with Onions, Green Peppers and Mushrooms laced with Sauce Bordelaise, served on a Bed of Rice

For Under 12 Appetites
Hamburger or Fish Sandwich
French Fries, Garnish

Prime Rib of Beef Au Jus
Slowly cooked in Rock Salt, served with Natural Juices.
Friday and Saturday only.

Beverages

Coffee . . . Special Blend . . . .

Tea . . . Hot or Cold . . . .

Milk . . . Grade A . . . .

Beer

Imported Mexican Dos Equis . . . .

Domestic . . . .

Dessert

Flan . . . .
Egg Custard topped with Carmel

Sherbet or Ice Cream . . . .

Pear Belle Helene . . . .

Homemade Cheese Cake . . . .
With Bing Cherries

Creme de Mint Parfait . . . .

River View Dining of the Nehalem River and Neah-Kah-Nie Mountain.

THE *Troller*

RESTAURANT & CHARTERS

THE Troller is the center of activity on Garibaldi's Fisherman's wharf, providing both year-round charter services and restaurant facilities. From their long and close association with the sea, the Vandecoevering family has developed a deep appreciation of and real commitment to the area, and they've created a restaurant responsive to the needs of this fishing-oriented community. The decor predictably reflects its setting, and dining is casual at any hour. The nautical motif is not overdone, and the atmosphere is one of simplicity and lack of pretense, appealing to all fishermen, young and old, real and "armchair".

The Troller
Fisherman's Wharf,
Moorage Basin Road
P.O. Box 408
Garibaldi, OR 97118

322-3666

Hours: April 1-October 15—24 hours
October 16-March 31
6 am-10 pm weekdays
24 hours weekends
Closed Easter, Thanksgiving, Christmas,
New Years

Libations: Beer and wine. Cocktails only during summer season

Payment: VISA, Mastercharge, American Express

Reservations: Not accepted

The Troller

A Wedding of Garibaldi Seafood & Tillamook Cheese Casserole

1 pound small seashell macaroni, cooked and drained
½ cup butter
½ cup chopped green pepper
¾ cup chopped onion
¾ cup flour
3 teaspoons salt
4 cups milk
½ teaspoon white pepper
1½ cups Tillamook cheese
1 lemon (juice of)
2 teaspoons prepared mustard
1 teaspoon Worcestershire sauce
4 tablespoons catsup
2 pounds of any combination of cooked Garibaldi seafood: crab, shrimp, fish, oysters

Combine the butter, green pepper, onion, flour, and salt. Cook until onion is transparent. Add milk, pepper, cheese, lemon juice, mustard, Worcestershire sauce, and catsup. Cook until smooth and bubbly. Stir in seafood. Pour into casserole and heat until very hot. Garnish with parsley and lemon slices.

The Troller
on Fisherman's Wharf

**RESTAURANT
LOUNGE &
CHARTERS**

Cocktails
- *Tillamook Oysters*
- *Dungeness Crab*
- *Garibaldi Shrimp*

Salads
- *Dungeness Crab*
- *Garibaldi Shrimp*
- *Tuna & Tomato*
- *Chef's Salad*
- *Tossed Green*
- *Salad Bar*

- *Clam Chowder (cup or bowl)*
- *Chili (cup or bowl)*
- *Soup (cup or bowl)*
- *Beef Stew*
- *Oyster Stew*
- *Mushrooms, deep fried*
- *Bucket of Steamer Clams*

Dinners
- *Tillamook Bay Oysters*
- *Salmon or Halibut Steak*
- *Grilled Razor Clams*
- *Prawns, batter-fried*
- *Scallops*
- *Fish Filets, Almondine*
- *Squid, Calamari*
- *Captain's Plate*
- *Lobster Tails (2)*

- *Steak & Shrimp*
- *Steak & Lobster*

- *Top Sirloin Steak*
- *New York Steak*
- *Liver & Onion*

VISIT OUR WINE AND SALAD BAR WHEN ORDERING DINNER.

Hadley House!

Tillamook, Oregon

ALL the charm reminiscent of another era permeates the Hadley House. Owners Harold and Betty Schild have captured the origins of this stately, early 1900's home in the restored decor and furnishings and the employment of antique pictures, lace curtains, and a cheery, glowing warmth. The separate rooms have now been converted into semi-private dining areas where patrons are encouraged to gather and linger. While the motif of this period restaurant may be turn-of-the-century, we think you'll find their fare nothing but up-to-date in diversity of selection and quality of preparation.

Hadley House
2201 3rd Street
Tillamook, OR 97141

842-2101

Hours: Summer 11:30 am- 9:30 pm Sun.-Thurs.
4:30 pm-10 pm Sat.
Winter 11:30 am- 9 pm Sun.-Thurs.
4:30 pm- 9:30 pm Sat.
No holiday closures

Libations: No alcoholic beverages

Payment: VISA, Mastercharge, checks with Bank Guarantee Card

Hadley House Carrot Cake

2 cups flour
2 teaspoons baking soda
2 teaspoons salt
2 teaspoons cinnamon
2 cups sugar
1½ cups oil
4 eggs
3 cups grated carrots
1 cup chopped nuts

Combine first 5 ingredients. Add the oil and mix well. Stir in eggs, one at a time. Blend in carrots and nuts. Pour into lightly oiled 13x9 inch pan and bake 1 hour at 350 °F.

Frosting

Beat until creamy: 1 pound box powdered sugar, 8 ounces cream cheese, 1 stick butter and 1 tablespoon vanilla. Stir in 1 cup coconut and 1 cup chopped nuts. Spread on cooled cake.

Welcome To Hadley House!

Tillamook, Oregon

We try to offer the finest cuisine, prepared for your eating enjoyment. We feature Tillamook County Seafood, Tillamook natural cheddar Cheese and dairy products from Tillamook's contented cows.

Salad Bar

The salad bar is included in the price of your meal. additional charge for second serving.
Salad Bar without meat...

Salads

Served with choice of dressing and warm bread.

CHEF SALAD............................
Fresh lettuce served with generous portions of turkey, ham, Tillamook Cheese, olives, tomato and hard boiled egg.

ONE HALF CHEF SALAD ....

SHRIMP LOUIE............................
Tiny pacific shrimp top this attractive salad.

CRAB LOUIE ....
Shredded lettuce artfully decorated with olives, tomato, hard boiled egg and lemon.

ONE HALF CRAB LOUIE.................
Just right for the light eater.

Hadley House Specialities

ROAST BEEF AND BROWN GRAVY.........
An old favorite served with a flair by people who care. Choice of baked potato or rice pilaf.

SOUTHERN FRIED CHICKEN ....
Our Oregon fryers cooked to a succulent crispy golden brown. Served with baked potato or rice pilaf.

FRESH SAUTEED CHICKEN LIVERS........
In mushroom sauce. Served on bed of rice.

VEGETARIAN PLATE.....................
Baked potato, onion rings, mushrooms, cottage cheese, and tomato slices.

ROAST TENDER CAPON..................
German style capon stuffed with sage dressing. Baked to a golden brown. German potato pancakes.

GRILLED PORK CHOPS...................
Grilled to a golden brown and served weith applesauce and savory dressing.

BREADED VEAL CUTLET ....
Tender veal served with a tasty cream sauce.

Steaks

Served with baked potato or rice pilaf.

HAM STEAK.............................
Delightfully spiced ham with a pineapple ring.

GROUND SIRLOIN ....
8 oz. topped with a deep fried mushroom.

MINI STEAK.............................
5 oz. tenderloin for the small eater.

FINGER STEAKS ....
Deep fried and served with teriyaki sauce.

RIB EYE ....
8 oz. topped with a deep fried mushroom.

NEW YORK...............................
10 oz. topped with a deep fried mushroom.

STEAK AND SHRIMP.....................
5 oz. steak with our fresh deep fried shrimp.

STEAK AND CRAB LEGS ....
5 oz. steak and deep fried crab legs.

Seafood

All dinners served with salad bar, choice of potato, or rice pilaf, and warm bread.

FISH 'N CHIPS . . . .
From local waters, served with French Fries.

GRILLED PACIFIC OYSTERS. . . . .
Served with tartar sauce and lemon.

STEAMED CLAMS . . . .
A delicacy of the house, served with drawn butter.

DEEP FRIED SCALLOPS. . . . .
Breaded and served with tartar sauce and lemon.

GRILLED HALIBUT STEAK . . . .
Served with tartar sauce and lemon.

BAKED PACIFIC SALMON STEAK. . . . .
Baked in white wine, served with tartar sauce and lemon. Grilled on request.

GRILLED PACIFIC RAZOR CLAMS. . . . .
Served with tartar sauce and lemon.

FRIED SHRIMP . . . .
In our chef's special breading, cocktail sauce and lemon wedge.

CAPTAIN'S PLATE. . . . .
A combination of your favorite seafoods; scallops, oyster, shrimp, and white fish.

DEEP FRIED CRAB LEGS. . . . .
Served with tartar sauce and lemon.

Appetizers

French Fries . . . .
Fresh Deep Fried Mushrooms . . . .
Fried Onion Rings . . . .
Combination — mushrooms, onion rings, fries . . . .
Tillamook Cheese and Crackers . . . .

Desserts

Our baker takes great pride in creating pastries, pies, specialty breads and other epicurian delights. Ask to see our dessert tray.

Flavor of the day ice cream . . . . .
Sherbet . . . .
Pie . . . .
Cheesecake . . . .

Beverages

Coffee, tea, milk, sanka, buttermilk, soft drinks or iced tea — Your choice

Classic Sandwiches

Complimented by tossed or potato salad.

Grilled Crab & Cheese or
Grilled Shrimp & Cheese . . . .
French Dip . . . .
Bacon, Lettuce & Tomato. . . . . . .
Cold Turkey Sandwich . . . .
Reuben . . . .
Club House on Toast. . . . .
Ham Wellington . . . .
Hamburger . . . .
Cheeseburger . . . .
Patty Melt. . . . .

Menu's available for children 12 and under.

May you find at the Hadley House the quality and glow of contentment that is given from our heart.

Your hosts,
Harold and Betty Schild

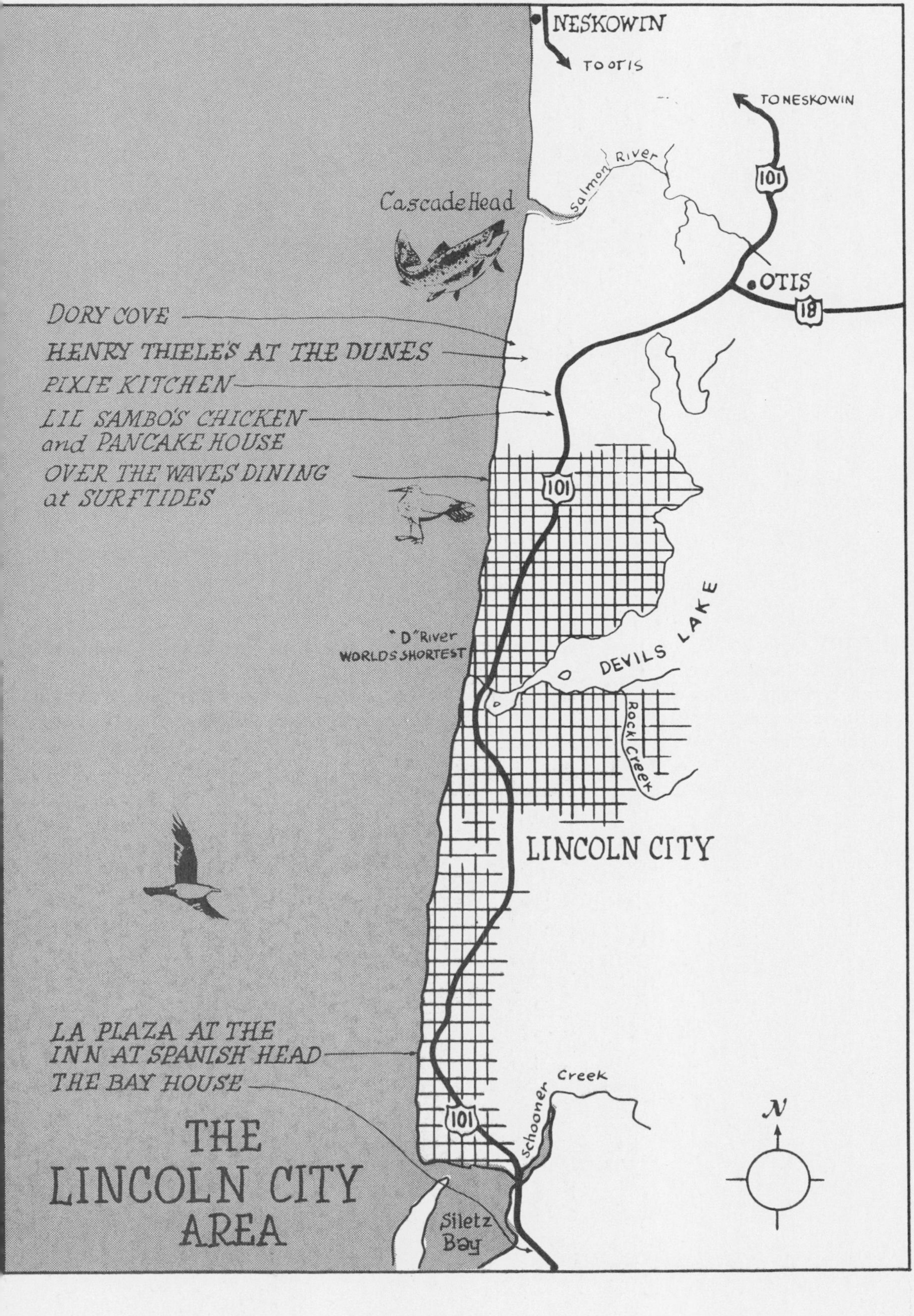

NESKOWIN
TO OTIS
TO NESKOWIN
Salmon River
101
Cascade Head
OTIS
18
DORY COVE
HENRY THIELE'S AT THE DUNES
PIXIE KITCHEN
LIL SAMBO'S CHICKEN
and PANCAKE HOUSE
OVER THE WAVES DINING
at SURFTIDES
"D" River
WORLDS SHORTEST
DEVILS LAKE
Rock Creek
LINCOLN CITY
LA PLAZA AT THE
INN AT SPANISH HEAD
THE BAY HOUSE
Schooner Creek
N
Siletz
Bay
THE
LINCOLN CITY
AREA

DORY Cove's a bit off the typical tourist's path but is certainly not to be missed; it's an authentic local favorite. This restaurant is strictly casual, with a cheery down-home approach personified in the character of its manager Roy Johnson. Dory Cove's an extension of Roy's exacting taste. His guiding touch is to be seen everywhere from the nautical decor to the flawless dishes that leave the kitchen. Let the winter gales blow, or the spring rains come, you're sure to feel right at home at Dory Cove with its cozy interior and magnificent view of Polly Rock and Cascade Head.

Dory Cove
Next to Road's End State Park
Off 101 North of Lincoln City
Route 2, Box 408
Otis, OR 97368

994-5180

Hours: 11:30 am-9 pm daily
Call for current hours

Libations: Beer and wine

Payment: VISA, Mastercharge, checks

Reservations: Not accepted

Dory Cove

Roy's English Style Battered Fish

1 pint buttermilk (cultured)
½ pint lager beer
1 cup flour
2 ounces butter, melted
½ tablespoon onion salt
¼ tablespoon garlic salt
½ tablespoon salt
1 teaspoon white pepper
½ teaspoon baking powder

Put buttermilk and beer into a large bowl. Whipping vigorously, gradually add flour until batter is smooth. Add seasonings, melted butter, and baking powder and whip. Allow to stand for approximately 1 hour before use. Cut fish (cod, red snapper, halibut, etc.) into strips approximately 4 inches by 1½ inches. Dip in batter for a light coat and deep fat fry at approximately 300 °F. until golden brown.

Dory Cove Specials

Clam Chowder .... Bowl Cup

Captains Plate ....
(Fish, Shrimp, Clam Strips, Oysters, Scallops)

Seafood Casserole, Ala Victoria ....
(Broiled Fish Fillet Smothered With Crab and Shrimp Meat, Scallops in Victoria Sauce)

Roy's Special Combination Platter ....
(8 oz. Tender Loin Steak Fillet with Shrimp, Oysters, Scallops and Mushrooms)

PILOT BOATS

Shrimp Cocktail .... Large Small
Crab Cocktail .... Large Small
Combo Cocktail .... Large Small

BUN FLEET

Dory Burger (¼ Lb. Pure Beef Burger) ....
Dory Burger W/Cheese.....................
Dory Burger W/Bacon ....
Dory Burger W/Bacon and Cheese.............
Trawler Burger.........................
(2¼ lb. Burgers w/American, Swiss Cheese & Bacon)
Grilled Cheese (Swiss or American) ....
Grilled Ham and Cheese Sandwich........
Chili Burger w/Cheese ....
Chili Dog w/Cheese.....................
Fish Burger.............................
Oyster Burger...........................
Shrimp Burger ....
Club Sandwich..........................
(Turkey, Ham, Cheese, Bacon, Lettuce and Tomato)

Add to price w/French Fries

Use Our Sandwich Bar To Build It The Way You Want It!

DINNERS

All dinners served with a choice of stuffed potato, O'Brien potatoes or Steak Fries, a choice of salad or Clam Chowder or soup of the day and garlic French bread.

DORYMAN'S NET

English Style Fish Dinner.................
Scallop Dinner...........................
Shrimp Dinner ....
Broiled Halibut Steak ....
Surf and Turf (N. Y. Steak and Shrimp) ....
Broiled Salmon Steak............... Small Medium Large
(Salmon According to Availability)
Salmon Fillets ... Sm. Med. Lg.
(Salmon According to Availability)
Beer Battered Crab Legs.................
Oyster Dinner...........................

LAND-LUBBERS FAVORITES

½ Fried Chicken Dinner ....
Broiled Hamburger Steak (10 oz.) ....
Broiled New York Steak (8 oz.) ....
Broiled Rib Eye Steak (10 oz.) ....
Broiled Top Sirloin Steak (8 oz.) ....
Hawiian Ham Steak......................
Grilled Center Cut Pork Chops.............
(With Mushroom Sauce)

DIET PLATES

The Menu items listed below are for the convenience of those who wish to restrict their caloric intake. Salads are served with either Italian or Catalina Low Calorie Dressing.

Broiled Fish (With Fresh Garden Salad).........

Broiled 4 oz. Beef Pattie..................
(With Fresh Garden Salad)

Broiled 6 oz. Rib Eye Steak...............
(With Fresh Garden Salad)

Fresh Garden Salad w/Dungeness Crab....

Fresh Garden Salad w/Shrimp............

SMALL APPETITES

The Menu items below are for the convenience of children and senior citizens with smaller appetites. Served with small Salad and garlic bread except when ordering Hamburger.

Fish and Chips..........................

3 oz. Hamburger and Fries................

Chicken and Fries........................

HEAVIER CARGO

Homemade Cheese Cake.................

Homemade Carrot Cake..................

Homemade Ice Cream Cake...............

Old Fashioned Apple Pie.................

Berry Pie..............................

Assorted Ice Cream & Sherbet............

OUT RIGGERS

French Fried Potatoes (Large Order).........

Fresh Garden Salad.......................

Stuffed Potato...........................

Onion Rings (Large Order)..................

Garlic Bread............................

CARGO NETS

All baskets served with
FRESH GARDEN SALAD & GARLIC FRENCH BREAD

English Fish and Chips...................

Fried Shrimp and Fries...................

Oysters and Fries........................

Scallops and Fries.......................

Clam Strips and Fries....................

Chicken and Fries........................

Barbacosa Sandwich and Fries............
(6 oz. Ribeye Steak on French Roll
with Cheddar Cheese and Au Jus)

Steak Sandwich and Fries...............
(6 oz. Tenderloin)

LIGHTER CARGO

English Style Fish and Salad.............

Chefs Salad..............................

Crab Seafarers...........................

Shrimp Seafarers.........................

Combo Seafarers (Crab and Shrimp)..........

DRINKING VESSELS

Coffee, Decaf, Cocoa, Tea................

Milk, Pepsi (Reg. or Diet), **7-Up,**
Root Beer.................... Lg. Sm.

WINE
(Ingelnook)

Rose, Colombard, Burgundy, Chablis

Glass **½ Liter** **Liter**

BEER

Henikens (Imported).................Bottle

English Bass (Imported)..............Bottle

Lowenbrau..........................Bottle

Miller...............................Bottle

Miller Light.........................Bottle

Olympia Tap.........................Bottle

Henry Thiele

At The Dunes

RESTAURANT AND CHART ROOM

THE family tradition of excellence in dining was brought to the coast by Henry Thiele in 1959. The move was a good one, for his arrival lent credence to the novel (at that time) idea that memorable dining was possible on the coast. That notion hasn't been forgotten since. Located at The Dunes Motel, the facility offers an inspiring view of the Pacific. The relaxing interior, with its complement of paintings, is in harmony with the setting. It goes without saying that the menu measures up to the atmosphere. Henry's sons, Henry, Jr. and Thomas, are now active in the business. Their personal touch and commitment are your assurance of an excellent meal.

Henry Thiele Restaurant at
The Dunes
1501 N.W. 40th
P.O. Box 247
Lincoln City, OR 97367

994-5255

Hours: 7 am-11 pm daily
No holiday closures

Libations: Full wine list, cocktails, and beer

Payment: VISA, Mastercharge, and
American Express

Reservations: Suggested

Henry Thiele Restaurant

Sole Marguerite

6-4 ounce portions of English sole
8 ounces Dungeness crabmeat
¼ cup chopped ripe olives
juice of ½ fresh lemon
1 tablespoon dry sherry
3 ounces cream cheese
hollandaise sauce
baby shrimp

Make a paste of the cream cheese, crabmeat, olives, lemon juice and dry sherry. Place mixture on piece of sole and roll up with skin inside. Bake with a little butter in 350 °F. oven for 12 to 15 minutes. Drain off butter, top with hollandaise sauce and baby shrimp. Serves 6.

FOR YOUR

Added Dining Pleasure

ENJOY OUR FEATURE COCKTAILS OR A BOTTLE OF WINE

"Golden Dawn"
(Vodka and Orange Juice Laced with Apricot Brandy)

"Henry's Marthiele"
(High and Dry Gin, Spanish Dry Sack Sherry—King Size)

"Martini or Manhattan In-A-Swirler"

"Deluxe Old Fashioned"

See Complete Wine List on Your Table

FULL COURSE DINNERS

CHOICE OF: Soup, Clam Chowder or Tomato Juice Cocktail
Tossed Green Salad with choice of Dressing; Baked Potato served with
Whipped Butter, Sour Cream and Chives or French Fries or Rice

Entrees

Assorted Sea Food Platter
Prawns, Oysters, White Fish and Scallops, fried golden brown. Served with tartar sauce.

Ocean Fresh Razor Clams
Lightly breaded and grilled to flavorful tenderness. Served with tartar sauce.

Fresh Salmon Fillets
Fresh from the Columbia, grilled and served with lemon butter.

Fried Jumbo Prawns
Ocean Garden Prawns, breaded and fried to a golden brown. Served with red sauce

Sea Food Au Gratin
Individually baked. A selection of sea foods delightfully prepared in Newberg sauce.

Grilled Chopped Steak
Choice, lean tender beef grilled to a turn and served with French fried onion rings.

Half Fried Chicken
Fresh Oregon fryers, disjointed and pan fried. Our own recipe. If you like chicken you'll love this

Prime Rib Au Jus
Choice beef served in natural juices. Rare, medium or well done, this can't be beat.

Captain's Cut

Veal Cutlet
Young veal, lightly breaded in our own mix. Served with mushroom sauce.

Dinner Steak
Choice 12-ounce steak, grilled to your liking.

Fish and Chips
Halibut strips, breaded and fried to a golden brown. Served with tartar sauce.

DESSERTS Princess Charlotte Pudding with Wild Cherry Sauce, Home-made Apple Pie, Ice Cream, Sherbet.

BEVERAGES Coffee Pot of Tea Milk
(No substitutions please)

Fisherman's Net

A "Variety Treat" From the Briny Deep
Broiled Baby Lobster Tail, Jumbo Crab Leg, Cove Oysters
Scallops, Prawns and White Fish, served with Salad.
Choice of Potato

Henry's Own Lobster Thermidor

EN CASSEROLE
Tossed Green Salad Baked Potato

Supper Suggestion

New York Steak Sandwich
Prime Rib Sandwich

Baked or French Fried Potato, Salad

King Neptune's Platter

Choice Tenderloin Steak
and
Broiled Baby Lobster Tail
Drawn Butter
Baked or French Fried Potato, Salad

Desserts

Princess Charlotte Pudding
Topped with Wild Cherry Sauce
Home-made Apple Pie
Cheese Cake
Strawberry Short-Cake, Whipped Cream
Chocolate Bavarian Cream Pie
Ice Cream or Sherbet
Sundaes

Beverages

Coffee
Pot
Pot of Tea
Milk
Sanka
Buttermilk

APPETIZERS

CRAB MEAT COCKTAIL, Red Sauce
FANCY FRUIT COMPOTE
BABY SHRIMP COCKTAIL, SUPREME
FRESH CRAB MEAT COCKTAIL, SUPREME
FRESH JUMBO CRAB LEG COCKTAIL

SOUPS

HENRY'S MANHATTAN CLAM CHOWDER
Cup Bowl

SOUP DU JOUR
Cup Bowl

FRUIT SALAD

Topped With Creamed Cottage Cheese
or Sherbet

JUMBO OREGON CRAB LOUIE

With Thousand Island Dressing,
Hot Rolls

CHEF'S SPECIAL SALAD

Tossed Green Salad with Julienne
Ham, Turkey, Swiss and American Cheese,
Asparagus Points and Tomato Garnish
Choice of Salad Dressing

Our Famous

ROAST

PRIME RIBS OF BEEF

AU JUS

Captain's Cut

A la Carte Entrées

Served with Tossed Green Salad, Choice of Dressing, Baked Potato, served with Whipped Butter, Sour Cream and Chopped Onions, or French Fries or Rice.

Fish and Chips
The freshest of fish, breaded and fried to a golden brown.

Baby Cove Oysters
Hand picked for flavor and freshness. Served with red sauce.

Choice Tender Scallops
Fresh from the sea, breaded and fried golden brown. With tartar sauce.

French Fried Jumbo Prawns
Ocean garden prawns especially selected for us. Served with red sauce.

French Fried Crab Legs
Jumbo Crab Legs at the peak of freshness. Served on toast with tartar sauce.

Assorted Sea Food Platter
The sea foods, golden fried and served with cocktail sauces.

Chinook Salmon Steak Filet
Fresh from the Columbia River, grilled and served with lemon butter.

Ocean Fresh Razor Clams
Lightly breaded, fried to tender goodness. Served with tartar sauce.

Ladies' New York Steak
Choice of beef, miniature in size. For men with small appetites too.

Choice Tenderloin Steak
Cut from the center of grain-fed beef. Melt-in-your-mouth flavor.

Broiled Lobster Tails (1) (2)
Fresh and flavorful. Served from our grill with drawn butter.

New York Sirloin Steak
Choice cut of tender grain-fed beef. Steak-eaters' delight!

Henry's Special Club Topper
Juicy cut especially selected by Henry Thiele. Try this.

Grilled Chopped Beef
Choice and lean, grilled to a turn and served with french fried onion rings.

Pan Fried Disjointed Chicken

We reserve the right to refuse service to anyone
Not responsible for lost articles.
Minimum service in dining room per person.

The Pixie Kitchen

THE Pixie Kitchen's a lively and entertaining place. Children of all ages are guaranteed to love it! There are crazy mirrors, a Ripley's Museum and game room, and an animated garden in the center of the restaurant. Maybe these are some of the reasons you'll often hear of land-locked Oregonians driving down to the coast simply to sup at Corrine and Harry Smith's Pixie Kitchen. The fun-filled surroundings blended with a reputation for quality, family-oriented dining have caught the attention of many notables, including Saturday Review and Ford Times. We're sure that you will agree the Pixie Kitchen's ideal for fun and food.

The Pixie Kitchen
3519 Highway 101 North
Lincoln City, OR 97367

994-2175

Hours: Winter 11:30 am-8 pm Sun.-Thurs.
11:30 am-9 pm Fri. and Sat.
Summer 11:30 am-9 pm Sun.-Thurs.
11:30 am-10 pm Fri. and Sat.
Closed the two weeks before Christmas

Libations: Beer, wine, and cocktails

Payment: VISA, Mastercharge,
American Express, Carte Blanche
and Diners

Reservations: Recommended year-round

Pixie Kitchen Red Sauce

2 cups catsup
1 tablespoon horseradish
½ teaspoon Worcestershire sauce
¼ teaspoon powdered garlic
¼ teaspoon powdered cloves
¼ teaspoon Tabasco sauce

Add all above ingredients together and mix until well blended. If you prefer a hotter sauce, add an additional tablespoon of horseradish. This sauce can be used for cocktail sauce or to accompany your favorite seafood. Makes 1 pint.

EVERY DINNER Includes — Salad Bar Service, Potatoes, Garlic Bread

When Reordering — No Food May Be Carried From The Premises.

With every dinner you are invited to help yourself from our ice cold salad and appetizer bar. Your waitress will serve you your main entree, garlic bread, and potatoes.

SEA FOODS

	Adult	Children 7 thru 11
OCEAN LING (Local—Golden Crust or Poached Creole)		
OCEAN COD—(A Delicious White Fish) Fillet Squares		
PERCH (Pacific Ocean)		
SOLE FILLET (Local)		
FRIED OYSTERS—From Tillamook Bay		
FRIED KING CLAMS		
DEEP SEA EASTERN SCALLOPS—Delicious		
FRIED RAZOR CLAMS (Local Delicacy) When Available		
HALIBUT FISH & CHIPS—(The Finest of all White Fish)		
SALMON (Caught Locally) This is Seasonal		
STEAM CLAMS—Small Clams—(Served with Drawn Butter)		
FRIED CRAB LEGS—Local—When Available		
FRIED SHRIMP (Large Prawns)		
COMBINATION SEAFOOD DINNER—Our specialty Halibut, Shrimp, Oyster, Crab Legs and Scallops		
BROILED LOBSTER (2 Lobster Tails)		
SALAD and APPETIZER BAR with garlic Bread		

Tiny Tot Dinners (6 years and younger) less than children (7 thru 11).

Because of the reduced prices—no reorders on children's dinners.

If dinners are shared, the waitress has been instructed to make an appropriate extra charge.
(no re-orders on shared dinners.)

Diabetic? Please Ask For A Special Menu.
Gift Certificates Available - Inquire At Front Desk

We feature Two Family Style Dinners that save both you and ourselves, time and money. These dinners are served Family Style to three or more people only. NO SUBSTITUTIONS ON FAMILY DINNERS PLEASE!

No. 1 FAMILY STYLE DINNER
Includes a combination of Ocean Cod, Oysters, Shrimp, Scallops, King Clam Section, Chicken.
For 3 or more people only.
No substitutions please.
Adults (Per Person) ....
7 thru 11 years (Per Child) ......
6 years or younger (Per Tot) ..

No. 2 FAMILY STYLE DINNER
Includes a combination of Halibut, Oysters, Crab Legs, Shrimp, Scallops, King Clam Sections, Chicken.
For 3 or more people only.
No substitutions please.
Adults (Per Person) ....
7 thru 11 years (Per Child) .....
6 years or younger (Per Tot) ..

A STATEMENT OF POLICY

Food costs, and especially fish and meat items, have escalated in price to an extent whereby we have changed our policy and still, with a slight additional charge, offer "all you can eat" to the few who feel they want more meat or fish. (At all times, the salad bar, potato and bread that is included with your dinner is "all you can eat" at no extra charge.

For example, if you wish to re-order on your main entree, this is how it would work: If you order shrimp, eat as much as you like from our salad bar. Then, your waitress will bring your main course in our usual generous manner of shrimp, with potato and garlic bread plus condiment. If you want more shrimp, your waitress will bring you another full order of shrimp and add one dollar to your guest check. Each additional re-order of shrimp would cost (Partial re-orders will be served at a reduced price and all re-orders must be consumed on the premises by the individual who re-orders). Unless you have a ravenous appetite, the original order of shrimp, fish, meat, etc., will generally be enough. (P.S. does not cover the cost of an order of shrimp, but it sure helps!

Corrine and Harry Smith

Crab Louie

SALADS

CRAB LOUIES A LA CARTE

(Local Crab)
With Garlic Bread
DUNGENESS

No Salad Bar

Clam Chowder

Clam Chowder (Milk Style) with Lots of Clams

Cup ....
Small Bowl ....
Large Bowl ....

Children's Orders

A LA CARTE PLATES FOR TINY TOTS

Ground Chuck Pattie ....
Fish and Chips .... Chicken (2 pcs) ....

Includes Potatoes, Bread, Beverage
The above does not include Salad Bar Service

CANNED JUNIOR FOOD AVAILABLE

Beverages

Milkshakes ....
Western Beer ....
Eastern Beer ....
Soft Drinks ....
Diet Soft Drinks ....
Tomato Juice ....
Tea - Sanka ....
Iced Tea ....
Milk 8 oz ....
Coffee—All You Can Drink ....
Buttermilk ....
Hot Chocolate ....
Chocolate Milk ....

These Dinners include the Salad Bar.

Meats & Chicken

Adult | Children 7 thru 11

Fried Chicken—Ranch Fresh ....
Suggested Wine—Rose

MEATS—Complete Dinner

Ground Chuck Steak with Mushroom Gravy ....
(with Onions Extra)
Pork Chops (two Thick) ....
Veal Cutlets ....
Top Sirlon Steak, 10-oz. ....
New York Steak, 12-oz. ....
Lobster Tail and 8-oz. Steak Combination ....

The dinners listed are not included in our re-order policy; Lobsters, Chops, New York and Sirloin Steaks as they are sold by number or weight.

A Word About Seafood

DEAR PATRON:

The Pacific Ocean offers some of the finest Sea Food in the World.

We try, when possible, to bring your favorite Local Seafoods to your table within hours of the time they reach the port.

Many times rough water or adverse fishing conditions leave us without your favorite dish.

Please forgive us, we do our best.

Thank you for your patience and patronage. We hope to see you again tomorrow.

HARRY & CORRINE SMITH

Side Orders

Cocktail - Crab - Oyster ....
Green Salad ....
Cottage Cheese and Fruit ....
Fruit Salad ....
Cole Slaw ....
Salad Bar Service with garlic bread ....
French Fries ....
Garlic Bread ....
Side of Vegetables ....
French Fried Onion Rings ....
Baked Potato (After 5 p.m.) ....

"EVER WONDER WHAT HAPPENS TO YOUR DOLLAR?"

We here at the Pixie Kitchen do our best to serve you good wholesome food, in a clean atmosphere, and in a courteous manner.

We try to do this at the lowest cost to you, and still keep our head above water.

We depend on volume in order to keep our prices as low as possible. We also know that if we can keep our prices low, our food and service good, that we can maintain our volume.

The chart on the right will tell you what happens to one of your dollars when it reaches our cash register. These figures come from our overall operation and it does not matter whether the dollar was spent on food, gifts, bar, printing or playroom.

Here is the break down:

Cost of Product	50c
Cost of Labor	28¾c
Utilities	1¾c
Supplies (Dishes, Silverware)	1¾c
Repair	¾c
Laundry, Cleaning & Upkeep	4c
Insurance	1¼c
Advertising	¾c
Licenses, Contributions	¾c
Dues-Legal-Int	¾c
Taxes	6¼c
Profit	3¼c
	$1.00

If we pay attention to business, work hard, and remain lucky, we should be able to hold the line. It's a very narrow margin between profit and loss.

Harry Smith
Corrine Smith

Buffet

BUFFET LUNCH
Monday thru Saturday
(Excluding Holidays)
(All you can eat)
Served from 11:30 until 2:30 P.M.
9 Hot Dishes 22 Cold Dishes
Adults ....
Children ....
1 thru 10 years—
Beverage Extra

We are proud to serve Darigold Dairy Products

Desserts

ICE CREAM ....
SHERBET ....
SUNDAES ....
PIE ....
PIE A LA MODE ....

Sandwiches

Cheese, Toasted ....
Tuna Fish ....
Hamburger, ¼ Lb. ....
Cheeseburger, ¼ Lb. ....
Chip Steak ....
Ham, Fried ....
Oyster ....
Clam ....
Crab, Bar-B-Q ....

French Fries Extra

Lil' Sambo's Pancake House

REMEMBER the story of Lil' Sambo who was tricked out of his colorful clothes by tigers? Well, Lil' Sambo's Pancake House has all the fun and fantasy of that tale. There are leopard-skin chairs, tiger-stripe lamps, palm trees and even Lil' Sambo himself peeping out from between branches. There are monkeys, counters of animals, and walls painted with jungle scenes. Ron Krieger opened his restaurant as only the third pancake house in the United States. It remains one of the best, and now offers hearty lunches and dinners as well. Kids will love Lil' Sambo's—and so will anyone who's even a trifle young at heart.

Lil' Sambo's
3262 North Highway 101
Lincoln City, OR 97367

994-3626

Hours: 6 am-8 pm daily
Closed half-day Thanksgiving and
all day Christmas

Libations: No alcoholic beverages

Payment: VISA and Mastercharge

Lil' Sambo's Marinated Salmon Barbecue

Use one-half of a 10-12 pound salmon, boned, skin on. Lay out flat in a large pan, cover with vegetable oil. Add:

juice of 6 fresh lemons
1 tablespoon dill seed
1 tablespoon Lawry's garlic salt
1 tablespoon hickory smoked salt
1 bunch green onions, diced

Marinate 12 full hours. Place at least 4 inches above charcoal, skin down, and cook until done, 40-50 minutes usually. The fish should not have to be turned unless it is an extra thick filet. Serves 8-10.

"LIL' SAMBO"

HAM OMELETTE
CHEESE OMELETTE
PLAIN OMELETTE
All with 3 Buttermilk Pancakes

When hash browns and toast are substituted for pancakes on these items there is a charge of   cents extra.

HAM & EGGS	With 3 Buttermilk Pancakes
HAM & EGGS	Hash Browns and Toast
BACON & EGGS	With 3 Buttermilk Pancakes
BACON & EGGS	Hash Browns and Toast
TWO EGGS	With 3 Buttermilk Pancakes
TWO EGGS	Hash Browns and Toast

SAUSAGE
Country Style & Eggs (Patty) With 3 Buttermilk Pancakes
With Links & Eggs With 3 Buttermilk Pancakes
Country Style & Eggs (Patty) Hash Browns & Toast
With Links & Eggs Hash Browns and Toast
CHOPPED HAM
SCRAMBLED EGGS With 3 Buttermilk Pancakes
CHOPPED HAM
SCRAMBLED EGGS Hash Browns and Toast

COFFEE (all you can drink) . . .
TEA . . . .
MILK . . . .
SKIM MILK . . . .
BUTTERMILK . . . .
POSTUM OR DECAFFEINATED .
ICED TEA . . . .
HOT CHOCOLATE . . . .
WITH WHIPPED CREAM

FRUITS & JUICES

ORANGE JUICE . . . .
GRAPEFRUIT JUICE . . . .
TOMATO JUICE . . . .
PINEAPPLE JUICE . . . .
V-8 OR APPLE JUICE . . . . . .
PRUNE JUICE . . . .
SLICED BANANAS & CREAM . . .
CANTALOUPE (In Season) . . . .
ONE-HALF GRAPEFRUIT . . . . .
STRAWBERRIES (Fresh Frozen) . .
PEACHES OR PEARS (Canned) . .
APPLESAUCE . . . .
PRUNES . . . .

PANCAKES

Light
BUTTERMILK

Old Fashioned
BUCKWHEAT

CORN (Meal)

POTATO
With 2 Bacon Strips

CLAM
With Lemon

STRAWBERRY
With Whipped Cream

HAWAIIAN
With Pineapple

Panama
BANANA

BLUEBERRY
With Hot Blueberry Sauce

COCONUT
Topped with Toasted Coconut

Our Specialty Whipped Tiger Butter

PANCAKES

FRENCH Pancakes
Rolled with Strawberry Jam

SWEDISH Pancakes
Served with Lingonberry Butter

JORDAN Pancakes
Rolled with Sour Cream

GERMAN Pancake
With Powdered Sugar & Lemon
(Allow 15 Minutes Extra)

APPLE Pancake
With Cinnamon Glaze
(Allow 15 Minutes Extra)

WAFFLES

TENDER GOLDEN WAFFLE

APPLESAUCE
With Cinnamon and Whipped Cream

STRAWBERRY
With Strawberries and Whipped Cream

BLUEBERRY
Hot Blueberry Sauce and Whipped Cream

SIDE ORDERS

HAM . . . .
BACON . . . .
COUNTRY SAUSAGE . . . . . .
LINK SAUSAGE . . . .
EGGS . . . .(1)   (2)
HASH BROWNS . . . .
TOAST . . . .
BUTTERHORN . . . .

THREE LITTLE PIGS IN A BLANKET
Link Sausage Rolled in Buttermilks

FRENCH TOAST
Powdered Sugar

CHILD'S PORTION
(Age Under 12 Years)
3 BUTTERMILK PANCAKES, 1 EGG
2 STRIPS OF BACON, MILK
OR
HASH BROWNS & TOAST, 1 EGG
2 STRIPS OF BACON, MILK

DOLLAR PANCAKES
6 CAKES . . . .
10 CAKES . . . .
18 CAKES . . . .

CEREALS
ASSORTED DRY CEREALS . . . . .
OAT MEAL . . . .
CREAM OF WHEAT . . . .

Lunch & Dinner Menu on Back Page
Served After 11:00 a.m.

Confused?

Try our Special Combination of Buckwheat, Corn, Coconut, Banana, Pineapple and Blueberry.
6 FLAVORFUL PANCAKES

Choice Top Sirloin Steak & Eggs
With 3 Buttermilk Pancakes

OR Hash Browns & Toast

Ground Beef Steak & Eggs
With 3 Buttermilk Pancakes

OR Hash Browns & Toast

LUNCH AND DINNER MENU

SANDWICHES

(served with Tossed Green Salad)

"THICK MILE HIGH" SANDWICHES

You Pick the Choice of One Each Meat Cheese & Bread

MEATS	CHEESE	BREADS
Ham	Swiss	Caraway Rye
Corned Beef	American	Sour Dough
Pastrami	Monterey Jack	German Black
Roast Beef		

All Sandwiches Served With Tossed Green Salad (Choice of Dressing)

"THICK MILE HIGH" FRENCH DIP

Served on French Roll With Tossed Green Salad & Lots of Au Jus

TIGERBURGER - 5-1/3 Oz. With Fries

CHEESEBURGER - 5-1/3 Oz. With Fries

The above Sandwiches are served with Lettuce, Tomato and Our Own Relish Mix

GRILLED CHEESE

CHILIBURGER

BACON & TOMATO

SCRAMBLED EGG

With Mayonnaise

DESSERTS

Pies Topped With Whipped Cream

CREAM & FRUIT PIE

Pie Ala Mode

ICE CREAM OR SHERBERT

SUNDAE

DRINKS

SOFT DRINKS

DIET PEPSI COLA

LEMONADE

MILK SHAKE

DINNERS

(Eat All You Want from Salad and Soup Bar) Fries, Baked or Whipped Potatoes and Chicken Gravy, Bread

DEEP FRIED SHRIMP

DEEP FRIED RAZOR CLAMS

OVEN BAKED SCALLOPS

OVEN BAKED FRESH OYSTERS

CHICKEN DINNER

Three Pieces Country Fried Chicken

FISH & CHIPS DINNER

GROUND BEEF STEAK

HAM STEAK

CHOICE TOP SIRLOIN STEAK

LUNCHEON SPECIAL

CHICKEN & FRIES

2 Pieces of Country Fried Chicken, Garlic Bread, Generous order of Fries

FISH & CHIPS

Three Pieces of Fish, Garlic Bread & Fries.

SALAD AND SOUP BAR

ALL YOU CAN EAT

SIDE ORDERS

CUP CHOWDER

LARGE CHOWDER

CUP SOUP OF THE DAY

LARGE SOUP OF THE DAY

BOWL OF CHILI

SIDE OF WHIPPED POTATOES AND GRAVY

SIDE OF FRIES

Robert Dumond's

Over-the-Waves

Surftides

A gazebo and semi-circle of ocean-front windows lined with hanging plants greet the visitor to Over-the-Waves Dining at Surftides Beach Resort. Owner Robert Dumond has brought a panoramic view of the Pacific Ocean into his full-service restaurant, directing spotlights to flood the surf at night and highlight the flocks of sandpipers in winter. Over-the-Waves Dining is a wonderful change of pace for special occasions such as group breakfasts, banquets, private dinner parties and receptions. We think you'll declare every visit and meal—breakfast, lunch or dinner—a celebration at Over-the-Waves Dining.

Over-the-Waves Dining at Surftides Beach Resort
2145 Jetty Street
Lincoln City, OR 97367

994-3877

Hours: 8 am-10 pm daily
No holiday closures

Libations: Full wine list, cocktails, and beer

Payment: VISA, Mastercharge,
American Express, and
personal checks

Reservations: Suggested

Over-the-Waves Dining

Blue Cheese Dressing

1 cup mayonnaise
½ cup sour cream
½ cup buttermilk
¼ pound blue cheese (crumbled)
1 tablespoon white vinegar
1 tablespoon lemon juice
¼ teaspoon garlic salt
¼ teaspoon coarse ground pepper
¼ cup finely chopped onion

Combine all ingredients in large bowl and stir well with wire whip. Makes about 2 cups of dressing.

PRIME RIB of BEEF AU JUS
Choice beef served with creamed horseradish

PEPPER STEAK - 8 oz.
New York steak sautéed with green pepper, onion, tomato and our chef's special sauce

STROGANOFF of BEEF
Tender beef in our own sour cream sauce with mushrooms, served over rice pilaf

HOT VEGETABLE PLATTER
Chef's choice of vegetables and cheese

SEAFOOD PLATTER
A combination of baked salmon, grilled halibut, deep-fried prawns and grilled razor clams — a collection of the finest in Pacific seafood

COMBINATION
6 oz. Petite Filet and (1) Australian Lobster Tail

VEAL MARENGO
Braised veal topped with prawns and brown sauce

FILET A LA OSCAR
Tenderloin of beef prepared in our chef's own sauce topped with asparagus and crab legs

BONELESS BREAST of CHICKEN SUPREME
Chicken breast, sautéed with vegetables and Supreme sauce served with rice pilaf

Appetizers

CRAB COCKTAIL
SHRIMP COCKTAIL
TOMATO JUICE

Salads

CRAB LOUIS
SHRIMP LOUIS
COMBINATION CRAB
CHEF'S SALAD
TOSSED GREEN DINNER SALAD

Soups

SOUP DU JOUR
Cup Bowl
CLAM CHOWDER
Cup Bowl

Entrees

All dinners include crisp dinner salad with your choice of our chef's special salad dressing or cup of soup du jour; rice pilaf, French-fried or baked potato; vegetable and fresh baked bread.

All Entrees are prepared especially for you. Please allow us appropriate cooking time. 20 to 30 minutes.

Pacific Specialties

FILLET OF SALMON - 8 oz.
Oven baked - topped with Hollandaise

SWEET & SOUR PRAWNS
A sauce specially prepared by our chef served on a bed of rice

SEAFOOD SUPREME EN CASSEROLE
Scallops, shrimp, crab, and halibut in special sauce, baked to perfection

GRILLED RAZOR CLAMS
In special egg batter, served with tartar sauce & lemon wedge

DEEP-FRIED PRAWNS
Chef's special batter and seafood sauce

SAUTÉED OYSTERS
Sautéed in white wine and butter with green onions, tomato, mushrooms and celery

SOLE AMANDINE
Tender fillets of sole grilled, topped with slivers of almonds in butter sauce

SCALLOPS MEUNIÈRE
Delicately sautéed in butter, wine and spices

HALIBUT STEAK - Grilled
Dipped in egg batter, served with lemon and tartar sauce

ALASKAN KING CRAB LEGS
A special Pacific treat served with drawn butter, seafood sauce and lemon

AUSTRALIAN LOBSTER TAILS (2)
Broiled to perfection (1)

From the Broiler

FILET MIGNON - 9 oz.
Wrapped in bacon

PETITE FILET MIGNON - 6 oz.
Wrapped in bacon

NEW YORK STEAK - 10 oz.

GROUND SIRLOIN - 8 oz.
Topped with mushroom sauce

the inn
at spanish head
RESORT HOTEL

La Plaza Restaurant

TUCKED into the side of a rugged cliff, high above the ocean below, La Plaza Restaurant at The Inn at Spanish Head offers its patrons a gull's eye view of the surroundings. Nowhere on the coast is there a more spectacular vantage point than here. But the show is not all outside the expansive windows. Diners relax ensconced in the warmth of traditional Spanish furnishings and rich colors as they sample Chef Chuck Phelps' tempting fare. When it's time for dining, you're sure to find La Plaza Restaurant to be a special part of your stay in the Lincoln City area.

La Plaza Restaurant at The Inn at Spanish Head
4009 South Highway 101
Lincoln City, OR 97367

996-2161

Hours: 8 am-11 pm May 1-October 31 daily
8 am-10 pm Nov. 1-April 30 weekdays
8 am-11 pm Fri. and Sat.
No holiday closures

Libations: Full wine list, cocktails, and beer

Payment: VISA, Mastercharge,
American Express, and Diners

Reservations: Strongly advised

La Plaza Restaurant

Veal Richard

1½-2 pounds boneless veal
¼ cup butter
1½ cups flour
6 ounces Dungeness crabmeat
6 ounces tiny shrimp
12 ounces heavy cream
4 tablespoons sherry
salt and pepper to taste
Tabasco sauce
1 lemon

Cut veal into thin pieces and pound. Season flour with salt and pepper. Dredge pieces of veal in seasoned flour.

In large skillet, brown meat in butter. Remove veal to a serving dish and keep warm.

On medium heat, add the sherry to skillet, stir to combine butter and drippings left from browning the veal. Add the cream and simmer 10-15 minutes until sauce thickens. Season sauce with salt and white pepper, plus dash of Tabasco sauce. Add shrimp and crabmeat to sauce and continue cooking just long enough to heat through.

Spoon sauce over veal and serve with lemon wedges. Serves 4.

WELCOME TO OUR HOME

We have prepared this menu for your dining pleasure. It is our sincere wish that you will enjoy your meal and will dine with us often.

The Chef

Appetizers

Shrimp Cocktail Supreme ....

Crab Cocktail Supreme ....

Oysters on the Half Shell ....

Bucket of Steamed Clams ....

Soups

Soup du Jour ....Cup Bowl

Clam Chowder ....Cup Bowl

Salads

MIXED GREEN, Choice of Dressing ....
French, thousand island, bleu cheese or our special house dressing

SHRIMP LOUIE ....

CRAB LOUIE ....

COMBINATION CRAB and SHRIMP ....

Vegetables

Vegetable du Jour ....

Sauteed Mushrooms ....

Desserts

Assorted Ice Cream or Sherbet

Cheese Cake ....

Creme de Menthe Parfait ......

Chocolate Sundae ....

Strawberry Sundae ....

Peach Melba ....

Fruit Pie ....
with Cheese or Ice Cream

Beverages

Coffee, Tea, Sanka, Milk or Soft Drinks ....

Enjoy One of Our Fine Wines Listed on Our Wine Menu

La Plaza Dinners

Includes Choice of Soup, Petite Shrimp Cocktail or Green Salad
Baked Potato, French Fries or Rice, Bread and Butter

CHOICE NEW YORK CUT ....

TOP SIRLOIN STEAK ....

FILET MIGNON, PRINCESS ....

SURF and TURF (Australian Lobster Tail and Tenderloin Steak) ....
Served with drawn butter

FILET MIGNON ....

STEAK SANDWICH ....

GROUND SIRLOIN STEAK ....

TURF and SEA ....
Princess filet plus choice of pan fried oysters or prawns

Our Chef Suggests

ROAST PRIME RIB OF BEEF au Jus ....

CONQUISTADOR CUT ....

From the Sea

GRILLED HALIBUT STEAK ....
Snowy white and firm fleshed, served with tartar sauce and lemon

ASSORTED SEAFOOD PLATTER ....
A delectable combination of prawns, salmon, scallops, halibut and oysters

DEEP FRIED PRAWNS ....
We bread our own and fry them to a golden brown

SCALLOPS, Saute Fine Herbs ....
Pacific scallops sauteed in butter with mushrooms and chablis, fine herbs

PAN FRIED OYSTERS ....
We serve petite Yaquina Bay oysters from our local waters

AUSTRALIAN LOBSTER TAIL:
One Tail .... **Two Tails** ....
Large succulent Australian lobster brushed with butter and lemon

BREAST OF CHICKEN NEPTUNE ....
Tender chicken breasts folded around a blend of dungeness and king crab, whitefish, herbs and spices

DUNGENESS CRAB LEGS ....
(When Available), sauteed in butter and Wine and served with toast points

PAUPIETTES OF SOLE ....
Filets of sole rolled and stuffed with shrimp and crabmeat, and topped with a flavorable wine sauce

BROILED FILET OF CHINOOK SALMON

For the Gourmet - La Plaza Specialties

OYSTERS LA PLAZA ....
Baked oysters, Spanish sausage, asparagus and cheddar cheese prepared in a savory Spanish sauce

VEAL CORDON BLEU ....
Veal stuffed with ham and cheese and topped with sauce supreme and mushrooms

BROCHETTE OF BEEF, Espagnol ....
Kebabs of beef, skewered with green peppers, onions and mushrooms topped with sauce diablo

PEPPERCORN STEAK LA PLAZA ....
(our own version), choice New York cut steak, broiled to order, topped with cherry tomatoes, green peppers, mushrooms and wine

THE SEAFOOD SKILLET ....
Scallops, prawns, crab legs and lobster sauteed in the serving skillet with shallots, mushrooms, fine herbs and white wine

BEEF LA PLAZA ....
Beef tenderloin cubes, mushrooms and shallots sealed in a crown of puff pastry, roasted to perfection and served on a bed of sauce bordelaise

"A Meal Without Wine is Like a Day Without Sunshine."

BAY HOUSE

RELAXED CONTINENTAL DINING ON SILETZ BAY

DAVID Hearing's Bay House is a new and worthy addition to the dining options available on the coast. Although only open for a short time, his restaurant has already garnered a following of those truly appreciative of his "clean" style of cooking: no overpowering sauces, only the freshest of foods presented in a straightforward manner. The menu is not lengthy, but David's skill and creativity are evident in each item. His unassuming touch is carried throughout the decor; the old house has been cautiously redressed to allow a relaxed view of Siletz Bay to filter through picture windows. Surely a fine restaurant in the making!

Bay House
5911 S.W. Highway 101
Lincoln City, OR 97367

996-3222

Hours: 5 pm- 9 pm Mon., Wed., Thurs.
5 pm-10 pm Fri.-Sun.

Libations: Beer and wine

Payment: VISA and Mastercharge

Reservations: Appreciated

Bay House
Oysters Sauté

14 medium small oysters
flour
clarified butter
¼ cup dry white wine
1 tablespoon fresh lemon juice
chopped parsley

Dust oysters with flour and sauté over medium high heat in butter. Turn when golden brown. Cook one minute longer.

Remove pan from heat and add wine and lemon juice. Return to medium heat and simmer two minutes. Sprinkle with parsley. Serves 2.

Appetizers

Bay Shrimp Cocktail

Baby shrimp served with cocktail sauce . . . .

Oyster Cocktail

Local young oysters and cocktail sauce . . . .

Snapper a la Bellwether

Pickled locally in Taft — served with sour cream or natural . . . .

Escargots Bourguignonne

Baked in garlic herb butter . . . .

ALL BAY HOUSE DINNERS ARE SERVED WITH FRESH VEGETABLES. RICE OR PARSLEYED RED POTATO. AND YOUR CHOICE OF SEAFOOD CHOWDER OR ONE OF OUR HOUSE SALADS TOSSED WITH
–CREAMY HERB DRESSING GARNISHED WITH BABY SHRIMP. OR
–VINAIGRETTE DRESSING TOPPED OFF WITH GRATED BLUE CHEESE

Cheese and Fruit Board

Available by request . . . .

A special assortment of freshly prepared desserts and pastries will be featured each evening

---

Bon Appétit

BAY HOUSE
5911 Southwest Highway 101
Lincoln City. Oregon 97367
996-3222

Open Nightly From 5 P.M.
Closed Tuesday

By special arrangement. BAY HOUSE
is available for luncheon parties.
meetings. and catering.

Entrees

Oysters Rockefeller

Served on the half shell in a bed of creamed spinach. laced with Pernod. and topped with Sauce Hollandaise . . . .

Fresh Fish of the Evening

David nightly prepares for you a different treat. fresh from sea or stream. . . . .

Oysters Sauté

Yearling oysters dusted in flour. sauteed in butter. white wine. and lemon. . . . .

Scallops Encasserole

Baked with fresh mushrooms. celery and herbs. with a delicate cream sherry sauce . . . .

Shrimp Crêpe

Baby shrimp blended with crisp vegetables. rolled in a crepe. and topped with Sauce Hollandaise. . . . .

Shrimp Salad a la Jeannette

We blend the shrimp with celery and a special creamy dressing and serve on a bed of lettuce with garnishes . . . .

Chicken Livers Lyonnaise

Freshly sauteed livers with mushrooms and onions in a delicate wine sauce. . . . .

Breast of Chicken Bay House

Oven roasted in red wine with onion. mushroom buttons. and fine herbs. . . . .

Steak Bearnaise

Ten ounce choice. pan fried in butter. with mushrooms and Sauce Bearnaise . . . .

Steak and Seafood Combination

Pan fried steak and your choice of Sauteed Oysters or Fresh Fish of the Evening . . . .

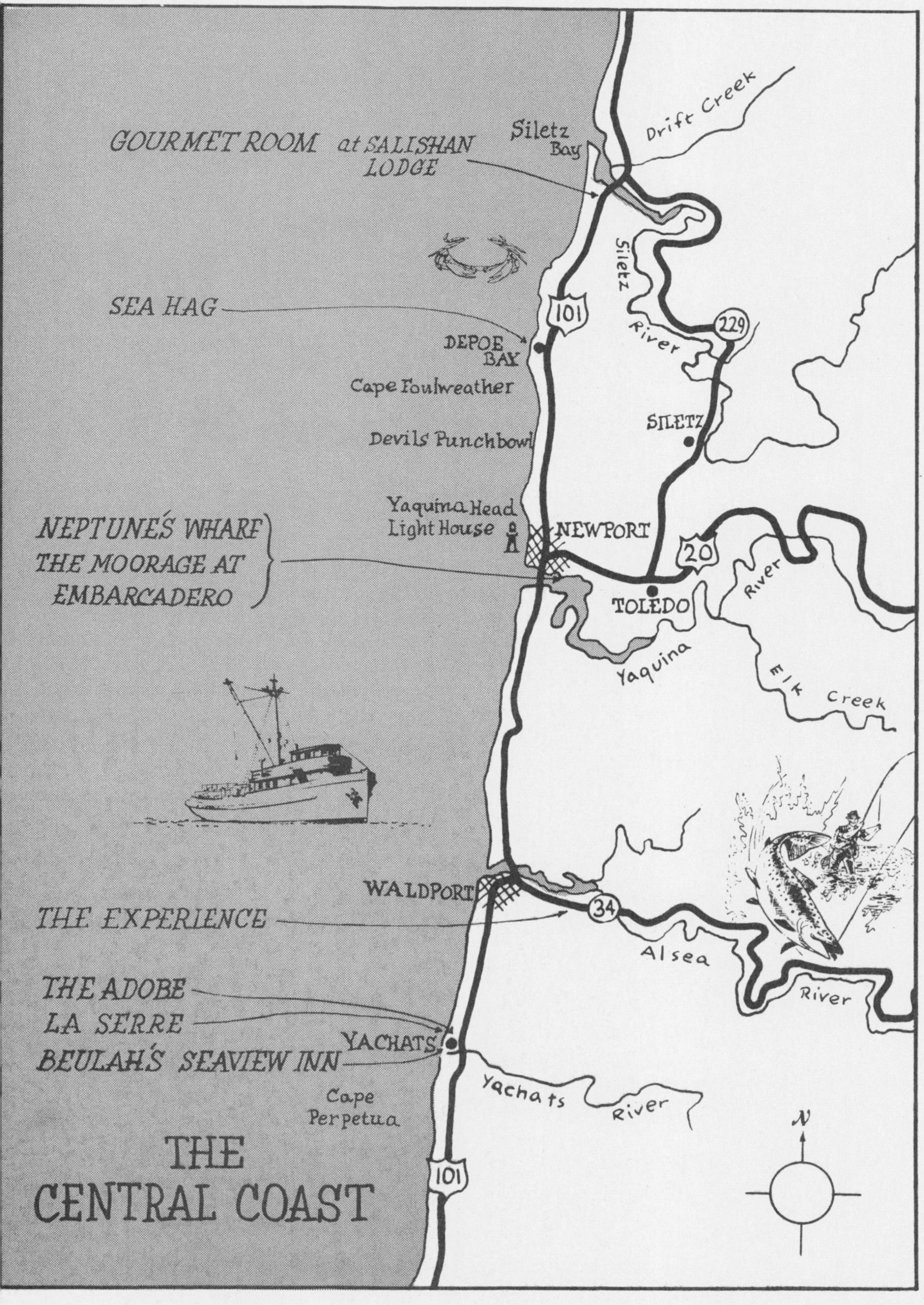

GOURMET ROOM at SALISHAN LODGE
Siletz Bay
Drift Creek
Siletz River
SEA HAG
101
229
DEPOE BAY
Cape Foulweather
SILETZ
Devils Punchbowl
Yaquina Head Light House
NEWPORT
NEPTUNE'S WHARF
THE MOORAGE AT EMBARCADERO
20
River
TOLEDO
Yaquina
Elk Creek
WALDPORT
THE EXPERIENCE
34
Alsea River
THE ADOBE
LA SERRE
BEULAH'S SEAVIEW INN
YACHATS
Yachats River
Cape Perpetua
N
101
THE CENTRAL COAST

Gourmet Room at Salishan Lodge

THE lure of the Gourmet Room at Salishan Lodge commences with one's initial contact with the classical decor and is rewarded by a memorable dining experience. An ambience of candlelight dining with intricately carved teakwood panels, fine linens, and lights shimmering on Siletz Bay framed with pine trees all heighten the mood pervading the Gourmet Room. The patron is enveloped in an atmosphere of tasteful, understated elegance, where waiters present the cuisine of Executive Chef Franz Buck with all the expertise of perfectionists. The winelist is among the most extensive we have ever encountered. The Gourmet Room ranks high on any list of fine restaurants.

Gourmet Room at Salishan Lodge
Gleneden Beach, OR 97388

764-2371

Hours: 6-11 pm daily
No holiday closures

Libations: Full wine list, cocktails, and beer

Payment: VISA, Mastercharge, Diners,
American Express, and
Carte Blanche

Reservations: Strongly advised

Gourmet Room Supreme of Chicken au Galliano

Select 4 good meaty chicken breasts—better yet, capon breasts. Debone and place between sheets of wax paper (one at a time) and pound carefully to an even size and thickness.

Stuffing (Can also be used for veal or pork dishes)

¼ pound butter, soft
¼ pound leaf spinach, parboiled and coarsely chopped
2 egg yolks, raw
2 shallots, chop finely and saute for a few seconds
1½ ounces Galliano
salt, white pepper, Accent, lemon juice

Mix all ingredients, adjust seasoning. Fill chicken breasts with about a tablespoon of stuffing. Carefully fold and shape breast. Stuffing must be enclosed! Chill.

Make mie de pain (white, dry bread crumbs) or use just plain bread crumbs. Beat 2 eggs and add salt.

Bread chicken breast: 1) flour, 2) egg-salt mixture, 3) mie de pain.

Use good cooking oil or clarified butter to brown breasts on both sides (saute pan or other flat and thick-bottomed pan). Finish in pre-heated oven at 375 °F. for 15-20 minutes.

This is a good dish for a dinner party—everything can be prepared a day or hours ahead of the actual serving time. The whole breast can be served, or it may be sliced and served on a bed of rice or noodles.

Appetizers

Cold:

OYSTERS ON THE HALF SHELL ....
A half-dozen select Oysters fresh from Oregon's Tillamook Bay. Many consider these Oysters equal in every way to the famous Eastern Blue Points.

FRESH MELON BALL COCKTAIL (In Season) ....

DUNGENESS CRAB COCKTAIL SUPREME ....

OREGON SHRIMP COCKTAIL SUPREME ....

CAVIAR
served with the proper embellishments
Sevruga Malossal 1-oz. ....
Golden Caviar of Canada 1-oz. ....

MARINATED HERRING ....
in Sour Cream

Hot:

CREPES AU ROQUEFORT, METAXA ....
Thin Pancakes with a Roquefort Cheese Cream Filling flavored with the famous Greek Brandy. Smooth and rich, highly recommended.

KÖNIGINPASTETE ....
A Patty Shell filled with Sweetbreads, Mushrooms, Veal and a special Cream sauce. Appropriately named "The Queen's Pastry".

SPANAKOPITA ....
A tempting Spinach Custard blended with Feta Cheese and baked between layers of Filo Pastry.

ESCARGOTS BOURGUIGNONNE ....

ARTICHOKES SALISHAN ....
Artichoke Crowns filled with Dungeness Crabmeat, topped with Bearnaise Sauce.

Soups

NEW ENGLAND STYLE
CLAM CHOWDER ....

CHICKEN CONSOMME
CELESTINE ....

CHILLED
CUCUMBER SOUP ....
Well Seasoned.

ONION SOUP GRATINEE .
Baked in the true French tradition.

Salads

WILTED SPINACH WITH CRISP BACON
(for two or more) ....

Prepared in our festive silver chafing dish at your table. The recipe remains with us, but we can reveal the basic ingredients — Olive Oil, Crisp Bacon, Lemon Juice and Piquant Mustards. A delightful blend.

CAESAR SALAD (for two or more) ....

EPINARDS A CRU (A Salishan Original) ....

Tender leaves of young Spinach finely cut into julienne strips, tossed with a true Continental Olive Oil, Vinegar and Russian-Style Mustard. Chopped Egg and Pimento complete the Garnish.

FRESH MUSHROOM SALAD ....

Sliced and prepared in the old-world manner.

SALISHAN TOSSED GREEN SALAD ....

Vegetables – Rice – Potatoes

IMPORTED SALSIFY ....

FRESH BROCCOLI ....

ASPARAGUS SPEARS ......

BAKED POTATO ....

WILD RICE ....

SALISHAN RICE ....

Beverages

Coffee Tea Milk Iced Tea Sanka

Salishan Specialties of the House

VEAL SWEETBREADS
Here at Salishan this delicacy can be listed as almost indispensible.

PRIME RIB OF BLUE RIBBON BEEF
Served au Jus, with Creamed Horseradish.

Full Cut (12-oz.) ....

Extra Cut (16-oz.) ....

RACK OF LAMB BOUQUETIERE (for two)
Broiled or oven-roasted Diable style.
The much enjoyed traditional presentation. Carved at your table and served with an assortment of Vegetables and Fresh Mint Sauce.

CHICKEN BREAST AU GALLIANO
Boneless Breast of Chicken with a Leaf Spinach and Butter filling, subtly flavored with Liquore Galliano. Lightly breaded.

MEDALLION OF VEAL SALISHAN
Milk-fed Veal topped with a delicate Brown Sauce, presented with a Crabmeat-filled Artichoke Crown glazed with Bearnaise Sauce.

ROAST DUCKLING A L'ORANGE
Prepared in the classic fashion
with Orange and choice Imported Liqueurs.

VOL AU VENT
Morsels of Tender Veal, Mushrooms, Sweetbreads and a special Cream Sauce, nestled in a delicate Puff Pastry Shell.

GRENADINES DE BOEUF AUX MORILLES
Thin Filets of Beef flamed in Brandy at your table,
glazed with delicate Sauce and topped
with the famous imported Morel Mushrooms.

(ALL ENTREES ARE AVAILABLE A LA CARTE — LESS)

From the Broiler

FILET MIGNON 12-oz., center cut

NEW YORK CUT STEAK 12-oz.

DOUBLE NEW YORK STEAK JARDINIERE (for two)
The well-liked "Entrecote Double" served with
our selection of Vegetables.

CARPETBAGGER STEAK
A Filet Mignon stuffed with a Pacific Oyster.
This Australian recipe is best when served medium.

DOUBLE CUT FRENCH LAMB CHOPS
Served with Mint Sauce.

CHATEAUBRIAND OF BEEF BOUQUETIERE (for two)
A double Filet Mignon, garnished with Vegetables.

Sauces and Butters

Hollandaise — Béarnaise — Madeira — Café de Paris Butter

From the Oceans

FILLET OF SOLE MARGUERY
This elegant dish includes Tiny Shrimp in a delicate, Creamy Wine Sauce.
Mussels and small Puff Pastry garnish the Sole.

OVEN-BROILED AUSTRALIAN LOBSTER TAILS
Served with Drawn Butter.

Two Tails ....

For a light meal: One Tail ....

LOBSTER THERMIDOR SERVED IN THE HALF SHELL
Diced Lobster, fresh Mushrooms and a perfect blend of Bercy and Béchamel Sauces. Topped with Cheese and browned under the broiler.

FILLET OF SOLE AMANDINE
Highly recommended!

DUNGENESS CRABMEAT "POMPADOUR" EN CASSEROLE
Baked in Wine Sauce and topped with Cheddar Cheese.
Supreme! Certainly one of our most favored dishes.

FILLET OF LING COD EN PAPILLOTE
This delicacy from local waters is garnished with tiny Oregon Shrimp then baked in Parchment to capture the subtle flavors.

CHINOOK SALMON FILLET
Oven-broiled in the distinctive manner expected of us.
Truly the King of Seafoods.

On the Light Side

A La Carte

A La Carte selections include Sourdough Bread Loaf.

FILLET OF SOLE MEUNIERE

OMELETTE AUX CHANTERELLES
With Herbs, Shallots
and Wild Mountain Mushrooms.

BREAST OF LEMON CHICKEN WITH FINE HERBS
Boneless Breast of Oregon Fryer, marinated in Lemon Juice,
with a Puree of Mushrooms, Shallots, Parsley, Chives and a hint of Tarragon.

PETIT FILET MIGNON
7-oz. Filet broiled to your liking.

ENGLISH CUT PRIME RIB (8-oz.)
Served with Horseradish Sauce.

Nouvelle Cuisine
MEDALLIONS OF VEAL NOILLY PRAT
Milk-fed Provimi Veal poached in Vermouth and topped
with Artichoke Purée. Served with a Crayfish garnish.

VEGETABLE PLATE
A selection of fresh and imported Vegetables
properly prepared and served piping hot.

SALISHAN SEAFOOD SALAD
This special Salad features Baby Oregon Shrimp and/or Dungeness Crabmeat
with Diced Tomato and Avocado on a bed of Alfalfa Sprouts and Lettuce.
Choice of Dressing.

Desserts

CARAMEL CUSTARD ....

COUPE NANTAISE ....
Fresh Strawberries and Orange Cubes marinated in Curaçao, Grand Marnier and Chartreuse over Vanilla Ice Cream.

CHEESE CAKE ....

ICE CREAM or SHERBET ....

FRESH STRAWBERRY FLAMBE (for two or more) .... Per Person

CREPES SUZETTE (for two or more) .... Per Person

BANANAS FOSTER (for two or more) .... Per Person

BRAZILIAN SNOWBALL ....
Coffee Ice Cream made in the old-fashioned creamy way, rolled in tasty Nougat — a mixture of Carameled Sugar and Toasted Almonds.

FRESH STRAWBERRY TART ....

MOUSSE ....

ICED ORANGE SOUFFLE GRAND MARNIER ....

A SUPERB SELECTION OF CHEESES .... Each 1-oz. portion
The finest selected imported and domestic offerings with appropriate Fresh Fruit.

PEACH A LA NELLY MELBA ....

After-Dinner Suggestions

COFFEE WELLINGTON ....
Piping hot Coffee with Rum, served with a Coffee-seasoned Whipped Cream float.

IRISH COFFEE ....
Salishan's own version of the world-renowned hot Coffee, Irish Whiskey and Whipped Cream combination.

COFFEE NUDGE ....
Kahlua Coffee, laced with Brandy and topped with Fresh Whipped Cream.

REMY MARTIN COGNAC ....

VANDERMINT ....

B&B ....

ORIGINAL SCOTCH ROCKER ....
A tempting blend of Scotch and Drambuie.

TIA MARIA ALPHONSE ....

BRANDY SEPARATOR ....
Kahlua, Brandy and Cream served over ice.

Special Occasions

Four to eight persons

We're pleased to help make your special occasion an evening to remember.
Preparation of these entrees is a process which requires the Chef's personal supervision.
Accordingly, we ask for at least 48 hours advance notice.

COULIBIAC
Filet of Chinook Salmon layered with Mushrooms, Rice, Onions, Shrimp and baked in a Pastry crust, served with Hollandaise Sauce.

VENISON BADEN-BADEN
Leg of New Zealand Deer, browned and braised in its own juices, served with Currant Jelly, Berny Almond Potatoes, Pear Half and Sour Cream Sauce.

FILET OF BEEF WELLINGTON
Roast Filet of Beef, medium-done and coated with Mushroom Forcemeat, wrapped in Puff Pastry and baked to a golden brown. Best served with Truffle Sauce.

ETHNIC AND INTERNATIONAL DINNERS:
Austrian, Dutch, French, German, Greek, Hawaiian, Indonesian, Italian, Japanese, Philipino, Russian, Scandinavian and Spanish.

The Gourmet Dining Room is available for parties of up to eight persons.
For larger parties we suggest a private dining room.

The

SEA HAG

Restaurant and Lounge

"In the Heart of Depoe Bay"

GRACIE Strom's Sea Hag Restaurant in Depoe Bay (the world's smallest harbor) reflects her colorful personality; it is a lively and boisterous place, usually filled with an eclectic mix of local salts and inlanders. Gracie frequently provides the floor show herself, taking position behind the bar and hammering out an accompaniment to traditional juke box favorites with spoons on strategically placed bottles with assorted horns, whistles and bells thrown in for good measure. Dining is informal but well thought out, with Chef Don Grindstaff's personal touch evident in each dish. Save the Sea Hag for a night you want to have fun and fine food.

Sea Hag Restaurant & Lounge
P.O. Box 278
Depoe Bay, OR 97341

765-7901

Hours: Summer 3:30 am-2:30 am
Winter 7 am-10 pm weekdays
7 am-11 pm Fri.-Sat.
Closed Christmas

Libations: Full wine list, cocktails and beer

Payment: VISA and Mastercharge

Reservations: Not accepted

Sea Hag Restaurant

Bobby Heuer's Clam Chowder

6 slices bacon, chopped
1 cup chopped onion
1 cup diced celery
2 large potatoes, chopped
4 cups each water and clam broth
4 cups chopped clams
2 tablespoons clam base
½ cup flour
butter

Cook bacon until crisp. Add onions and cook until tender. Add celery, potatoes, water and clam broth. Cook until tender. Add clams and clam base. Cook 5 minutes. Thicken with flour combined with a little cold water. Stir into clam mixture and bring to boil. To serve, add enough hot milk to desired consistency. Top individual bowls with butter and serve 4 people.

SEA HAG FARM DINNERS

"ALL OUR BEEF IS U.S. CHOICE"

THICK NEW YORK STEAK 12 OZ.
Mansized and Broiled with Fresh Sauteed Mushrooms . . . .

GROUND CHUCK STEAK W/Mushrooms . . . .

ROAST SIRLOIN OF BEEF . . . .

PLUMP GOLDEN FRIED CHICKEN. . . . .

Farm Dinners Served With Rice or Potato, Loaf of Bread & "Build Your Own Salad"

★ ★ ★ ★ ★ EXCELLENT ANY TIME ★ ★ ★ ★ ★

HOT CHILI OUR OWN RECIPE . . . . CUP GIANT BOWL

CHICKEN BASKET GARLIC BREAD — FRIES . . . .

FRENCH DIP SANDWICH OPEN FACE FRENCH LOAF, AU JUS & FRIES . . . .

VEGETARIAN POCKET SANDWICH
Avocado, Cheese, Tomato, Sprouts, Served with Fresh Fruit . . . .

LO-CAL DELIGHT
Lean Ground Beef Patty, Cottage Cheese, Sliced Tomato, Rye Crisp
OR
Tuna & Shrimp Stuffed Tomato, Cottage Cheese, Rye Crisp . . . .

CHEF'S CHOICE STEAK SANDWICH
With Build Your Own Salad — Ranch Fries. . . . .

SEA HAG'S FAMOUS BOAT SALAD BAR
ALL YOU CAN EAT — BUILD YOUR OWN SALAD

SEA HAG'S DUNGENESS CRAB & CHEESE
Served Open Faced on English Muffin
Crawlin' with Crab Meat and
Smothered with Tangy Cheese Sauce

SANDWICHES

HAMBURGER "¼ lb. Ground Beef" . . . .
CHEESE BURGER "¼ lb. Ground Beef" . . .
CHILI BURGER Mounds of Cheese & Onions .
FISH BURGER Deep Fried White Fish . . . . . .
CLAM BURGER . . . .

ROAST BEEF . . . .
HAM . . . .
BAR-B-QUE HAM OR BEEF. . . . .
TUNA FISH . . . .
BACON & TOMATO . . . .

Sandwiches Served w/Potato Chips & Pickles — Choice of Rye,
Black, Hillbilly, or Pocket Bread — Fries or Potato Salad Extra

HOT ROAST BEEF SANDWICH
—OLD TIME FAVORITE— w/Gravy & Mashed Potatoes . . . .

COTTAGE CHEESE / FRESH FRUIT
Served in Giant Seashell . . . .

SMOKED SALMON
With Bagel & Cream Cheese
Served with Potato or Cabbage
Salad or Fresh Fruit . . . .

SIDE ORDERS

COTTAGE CHEESE. . . . .
FRIED POTATOES. . . . .
BAKED POTATOES w/Trimmins' . . . .

SAUTEED FRESH MUSHROOMS . . . . .
GARLIC BREAD BASKET . . . .
POTATO SALAD . . . .

BEVERAGES

COFFEE. . . . .
POT OF TEA . . . .

HOT CHOCOLATE With Whipped Cream. . . . . .
SOFT DRINKS . . . .

MILK OR BUTTERMILK . . . . LARGE GLASS. . . . . . .

SEAFOOD SO FRESH THE OCEAN HASN'T MISSED IT YET!!

BAKED FILLET OF SOLE IN WINE
STUFFED WITH CRAB & SHRIMP
With "THE WORKS"
GOURMET DELIGHT. . . . .

SAUTEED GIANT SCAMPI
HUGE PRAWNS SAUTEED TO
SUCCULENT PERFECTION
WITH EXOTIC HERBS & WINE
AND "THE WORKS"
DE-E-ELICIOUS. . . . .

SEA HAG SPECIAL
"FISHERMEN'S CATCH OF THE DAY'
ASK YOUR WAITRESS ABOUT
THIS OUTSTANDING TREAT

SCAMPI & STEAK . . . .
OUR SAUTEED SCAMPI WITH
A CHOICE BROILED STEAK
OR
LOBSTER & STEAK . . . . . .
A TREAT FOR THE HEARTY EATERS
WITH "THE WORKS"

"THE WORKS" *SEAFOOD DINNERS SERVED WITH RICE OR POTATO, LOAF OF BREAD & BUILD YOUR OWN SALAD*

★ **DEEP FRIED JUMBO SHRIMP**
OUR OWN SPECIAL BATTER
WITH "THE WORKS"

★ ★ **SEA HAG PLATTER**
SEAFARER'S SELECTION
FROM THE BRINY DEEP
WITH "THE WORKS"

★ ★ ★ **DEPOE BAY CRAB LEGS**
DUNGENESS CRAB LEGS
SAUTEED OR DEEP FRIED
WITH "THE WORKS"

★ ★ ★ ★ **GRILLED DEPOE BAY SALMON**
PRIZE OF THE NORTHWEST
WITH "THE WORKS"

OLD TIMERS SEA HAG FAVORITES

BAKED OYSTERS OR STEAMED BUTTER CLAMS
A TREAT YOU WILL REMEMBER
ALA CARTE WITH "THE WORKS"

SAUTEED HALIBUT CHEEKS
OR
SAUTEED SUCCULENT SCALLOPS
ALA CARTE WITH "THE WORKS"

★ ★ ★ **SEA HAG CREAMY CLAM CHOWDER**
OUR OWN RECIPE SELECTED BY
NEW YORK TIMES COOKBOOK
AS THE VERY BEST
CUP LARGE BOWL

OYSTER STEW
SWIMMING WITH OYSTERS

GIANT SEAFOOD COCKTAILS
★ OREGON SHRIMP
★ DUNGENESS CRAB

CLAM STRIPS W/GARLIC BREAD

★ **LOBSTER TAIL**
WITH LEMON & MELTED BUTTER
A SEAFARER'S PRIDE
WITH "THE WORKS"

★ ★ **RAZOR CLAMS**
TENDERLY GRILLED
WITH "THE WORKS"

★ ★ ★ **GRILLED OYSTERS**
GATHERED DAILY FROM
YAQUINA BAY
WITH "THE WORKS"

★ ★ ★ ★ **BAKED DUNGENESS CRAB/SHRIMP**
AU GRATIN WITH TASTY CREAM
SAUCE DELICATELY LACED
WITH WINE & "THE WORKS"

GRACIES
AVOCADO SALAD
STUFFED WITH SHRIMP
GARNISHED W/FRESH FRUITS
AND
CUP OF OUR FAMOUS
CLAM CHOWDER

SHRIMP BOAT
OR
SHRIMP AND FRIES
BATTER DIPPED JUMBO SHRIMP
GARLIC BREAD

FISH and FRIES
BATTERED WHITE FISH
GARLIC BREAD

SEA HAG
LOUIES
SERVED IN GIANT SEASHELL
SHRIMP

CRAB OR
COMBINATION

FOR A FINALE TO YOUR DINNER MAY WE SUGGEST

★ **BLACKBERRY TART**
WITH WHIPPED CREAM OR ICE CREAM
OUR RECIPE ALSO SELECTED FOR
NEW YORK TIMES COOK BOOK

★ **GIANT STRAWBERRY SHORTCAKE**
(IN SEASON) WITH WHIPPED CREAM OR ICE
CREAM & OUR OWN SHORTCAKE

★ **ASK WAITRESS ABOUT OUR OWN BAKED PASTRIES**

SEE OUR WINE MENU TO ROUND OUT YOUR MEAL

REMEMBER!!
OUR FRIDAY NIGHT
"ALL YOU CAN EAT"
STEAMED CLAM FEAST
AND
OUR POPULAR SUNDAY
CHAMPAGNE BRUNCH

Neptune's Wharf

NEPTUNE'S Wharf is the center of interest in Old Town Newport. Adjacent is the antique sailing ship, Sara, now fully restored and made into a maritime museum by owners Robert and Elaine Baker. In the summer months there are a multitude of sea birds that linger nearby. Inside the restaurant, the customer is treated to an extensive collection of paintings, encompassing local artists as well as artists from 16 foreign countries. The restaurant, a favorite spot for travelers, is a blend of properly formal sophistication and restrained elegance. You owe it to yourself to discover the delicious secrets of Neptune's Wharf.

Neptune's Wharf
325 S.W. Bay Boulevard
Newport, OR 97365

265-2532

Hours: Summer 11 am-10 pm daily
Winter 11 am-9 pm daily
Closed Thanksgiving and Christmas

Libations: Full wine list, cocktails, and beer

Payment: VISA and Mastercharge

Reservations: Suggested

Neptune's Wharf Shrimp Broil

Melt 3 tablespoons butter in sauce pan, add ¼ cup flour. Cook slowly to make a roux.

Remove from heat, add 1 tablespoon of chicken base, 2 cups of milk, white pepper, and salt to taste. Simmer slowly over low heat, stirring constantly, to make a rich sauce.

When thickened, add 1 tablespoon of prepared mustard and a teaspoon of horseradish, ½ cup of canned mushrooms, drained. Simmer for a minute or two. Add tiny Pacific shrimp and slowly simmer till shrimp are hot.

Serve on 4 split and toasted English muffins. Portions for 4 people.

Appetizers

	Small	Large
Crab Cocktail		
Tiny Peacock Shrimp Cocktail		
Yaquina Bay Oyster Cocktail		

Soups

Boston Clam Chowder *(Our Own Special Recipe)*
Yaquina Bay Oyster Stew *(Rich, Creamy)*
Soup du Jour .... Cup .... Bowl

Salads

Crab Louis
Garnished with hard cooked eggs, sliced tomatoes and olives.

Tiny Peacock Shrimp Louis

Combination Crab & Shrimp Louis

Chef's Salad
Julienne strips of ham, chicken, cheese on lettuce, garnished with hard cooked eggs, sliced tomatoes, pickles and olives.

Crab Salad or Shrimp Salad
Crab or shrimp and mayonnaise, garnished with tomato.

Cottage Cheese and Fruit

Fresh Fruit Salad
Delectable assortment of fresh fruits according to season. Topped with ice cream or whipped cream.

Family Budget Specials

Neptune's Hot Shrimp Broil
Toasted split English muffin topped with tiny shrimp and zesty sauce.

Shrimp Au Gratin
Shrimp in a creamy cheese sauce on toasted split English muffin.

Hamburger (A Full Meal)
Cheeseburger (A Bigger Meal)
Peanut Butter & Jelly

Desserts

Ice Cream
Sherbet
Homemade Pies (Baked Daily)
a la mode

Fresh Fruit (Only In Season)
With Heavy Cream or Whipped Cream
With Ice Cream

Beverages

Coffee .... **Milk**
Tea .... **Sanka**

Land & Sea

Dinner For Two
Choice Top Sirloin Steak & Steamed Little Neck Clams In Shell Served En Casserole.
Tossed Green Salad, Baked Potato, Dessert, Beverage

Dinner For Two With Wine

Brunch

Served from 11:00 a.m. to 12:30 p.m. only

Eggs Benedict
Two poached eggs on English muffins and ham with Hollandaise sauce.

Country Brunch
Two eggs, hash browns, bacon or ham, toast.

Crepes Parisienne
Thin French pancakes, rolled with melted butter and powdered sugar.

Cappuccino • Cafe de Vita
Coffee, chocolate and spices with whipped cream and chocolate curls.

Plain
With Brandy
With Vandermint

Lake Country Wines

Taylor's **New York**
White, Gold, Pink or Red

Glass
Carafe (for two)

Sangria .... Large Pitcher
Red wine, fruit juices and fresh fruit. Small Pitcher

Copa-Da-Vino .... Large Pitcher
White wine, fruit juices and fresh fruit. Small Pitcher

Imported and California wines and cocktails of your choice are available from
The Dolphin Room

Seafood Dinners

(Fresh seafood subject to season and weather conditions)

Dinners include choice of clam chowder or green salad, baked potato or french fries.
A la carte includes entree' with baked potato or french fries.

A la Carte Dinner

Lobster Tail ....
Steeped in wine and served on the half shell with lemon and hot butter.

Pacific Halibut Steak ....
Brushed with butter and broiled. Served with lemon wedges.

Petrale Sole ....
With tarragon butter, egg-dipped, then dusted with fine cracker crumbs. Served with lemon and tartar sauce.

Razor Clams ....
Selected clams slightly breaded, cooked quickly for tenderness, served with tartar sauce and lemon.

Pacific Oysters ....
Served on a nest of chopped lettuce, with tartar sauce.

Crab Delmonico En Casserole ....
Select crab meat served in rich supreme sauce, topped with cheese.

Crab Curry Indienne ....
With chutney and assorted condiments.

Tiny Shrimp Curry Indienne ....
With chutney and assorted condiments.

Each of the above served with rice

Yaquina Bay Oysters ....
Pan-fried in butter.

Hangtown Fry ....
Small selected Yaquina oysters, sautéed in butter then folded into beaten eggs under the broiler.

Steamed Little Neck Clams In Shell ....
Steamed and served en casserole with lemon nectar and melted butter.

Scampi ....
Tenderly steamed in the shell, served with drawn butter and lemon.

Bouillabaisse Marseillaise ....
An assortment of succulent seafoods simmered in a secret savory sauce served en tureen.
Green garden salad and garlic bread served with this specialty.

★ **Fish and Chips** ....

★ **Atlantic Scallops** ....
Served on chopped greens with tartar sauce and lemon wedges.

★ **Jumbo Prawns** from Ocean Gardens ....
Served on a nest of greens with tangy hot sauce and lemon.

★ **The Clipper Ship Seafood Platter** ....
An assorted platter of jumbo shrimp, scallops, ling cod and oysters.
Served on a nest of greens with tangy hot sauce and lemon.

From The Broiler

Choice Thick Top Sirloin Steak (13-oz.) ....
Served with crisp onion rings.

Top Sirloin Steak (8-oz.) ....
Served with crisp onion rings.

Surf & Turf — Lobster & Steak ....
One lobster tail served en shell and steak brochette.

★ **Available in Child's Portions** ....

A Village Green Resort Motor Hotel & Marina

EMBARCADERO

The Moorage at Embarcadero

Skirting the waterfront in Newport's Old Town is the region's only marina-resort, Embarcadero. Here is located The Moorage restaurant. Lavish in the use of natural woods, this waterfront establishment acts as an observation platform for all the doings here in Yaquina Bay. As patrons feast amidst the contemporary surroundings, the bustling movements of the waterfront go on unceasingly outside. The facility's crisp decor draws in the excitement of the bay and successfully pairs it with its own restrained nautical motif and properly executed menu. It's quite obvious that The Moorage has come a long way towards its goal of being "the best on the coast".

The Moorage at Embarcadero
1000 S.E. Bay Blvd.
P.O. Box 1067
Newport, OR 97365

265-8521

Hours: 7 am-10 pm daily
No holiday closures

Libations: Full wine list, cocktails, and beer

Payment: VISA, Mastercharge,
American Express, and
Carte Blanche

Reservations: Suggested

The Moorage
Crab Meat Casserole

½ cup onions, finely chopped
2 tablespoons butter
2 tablespoons flour
1 cup clam juice
1½ cups tomatoes, finely diced
½ cup green peppers, coarsely diced or chopped
2 tablespoons parsley, chopped fine
¼ cup mushrooms,
sliced and sauteed prior to adding
¼ cup green olives, sliced
1 teaspoon salt (to taste)
½ teaspoon black pepper
⅛ teaspoon thyme
2 tablespoons Worcestershire sauce
1 pound cooked crab meat
cheese sauce

Sauté the ½ cup onions in the butter until transparent. Add flour and cook until it starts to turn brown. Add clam juice, stirring constantly. Add diced tomatoes, green peppers, parsley, green olives, salt, pepper, thyme, and mushrooms. Simmer about 10 minutes to allow flavors to blend.

Add 2 tablespoons Worcestershire sauce and 1 pound crab meat. Pour into 2-quart casserole and top with melted cheese sauce (cheddar cheese is recommended).

Bake at 350 °F. for about 15 minutes or until golden brown.

Appetizers

TINY BAY SHRIMP COCKTAIL
OYSTERS ON THE HALF SHELL
CLAMS ON THE HALF SHELL
DUNGENESS CRAB COCKTAIL

Soups 'N Stews

CLAM CHOWDER /cup ... / bowl ...
SOUP DU JOUR /cup ... / bowl ...
OYSTER STEW / bowl ...

Salad Dory

Make your own selection
from fresh seasonal greens
and garnishes

Seafood selections

CAPTAIN'S PLATTER
The captain's selection of native seafoods

SHRIMP PROVENCALE
Gulf Shrimp sauteed in garlic butter sauce with rice

STEAMED CLAMS IN A BUCKET
Fresh local steamers in their own broth
served with drawn butter

STUFFED LING COD
Oregon cod with Shrimp and Crab stuffing

BOUILLABAISE
Local seafood simmered with Wine & Saffron
in fish stock

FILLET OF SOLE
Sauteed in butter and almonds

THE CHEF'S FAVORITES

Crab Diable

Whole native Dungeness Crab
stuffed with Crab and Shrimp meat
and finished with a fine Diable Sauce

Five Star Salmon

Native coastal Salmon prepared
in three delicious fashions — your choice:
Norwegian-style with dill weed and diced tomato
Broiled fillet served tastefully naked
Poached with Hollandaise Sauce

The best of the rest

ROAST PRIME RIB of BEEF
Aged rib of beef roasted daily
with Yorkshire pudding

FILET WELLINGTON
Petite filet wrapped in pastry shell
with pate' and mushrooms

NEW YORK SIRLOIN STEAK
Aged sirloin served with maître d' butter

CHOPPED SIRLOIN STEAK
Made with the freshest ground sirloin

FISHERMAN'S BEND

PORTERHOUSE STEAK
Charbroiled to your order

SOME OF THIS 'N THAT
Brochette of Beef tips and Shrimp
with cherry tomatoes and mushroom caps

CORNISH GAME HEN
Stuffed with wild rice & finished with white wine

PORK LOIN CHOPS
Two thick juicy center-cut chops
served with hot spiced apple slices

All the above entrees include a trip to our Salad Dory,
Vegetable du Jour and choice of Baked Potato or our famous Steak House Fries

The Experience

Fine Dining

THE good news from the Waldport area is that founders Janice Willinger and Betty Hoffmaster are back in charge at The Experience, after a year's sabattical. Chef Janice's uncompromising approach to seafood cookery stresses that no short cuts can be taken; nothing is fried or battered, only pure creamery butter is used, and only the freshest and finest ingredients are offered. Desserts (if you still have room) are prepared with corresponding flair, with Cashew Kumquat Pie a typical example. The Experience has a new and slightly more formal look now, too, having undergone a major interior remodeling. But the food remains the major attraction here; you won't be disappointed!

The Experience
3750 Highway 34, 3 miles east of Waldport
Waldport, OR 97394

563-3568

Hours: Open 5 pm daily except Sun.
Open 1 pm Sun. Closed Tues. in
summer, Mon. and Tues. in winter
Closed Thanksgiving and Christmas

Libations: Full wine list, cocktails and beer

Payment: Checks, VISA, Mastercharge, and
American Express

Reservations: Suggested because of variable
closing hour and limited seating
capacity

The Experience Sturgeon Filbertine

½ cup teriyaki sauce
¼ cup Mirin (sweet rice wine)
2 teaspoons sesame oil
2 teaspoons minced fresh ginger root
1 clove garlic, mashed
sturgeon steaks, ¾-1 inch thick
chopped filberts

Mix first 5 ingredients to make marinade in glass or stainless steel bowl. Marinate at least 4 hours, turning occasionally.

Remove steaks and roll in filberts. Place steaks in shallow casserole in single layer.

Bake in 400 °F. preheated oven for 15-20 minutes.

The Experience

We serve complete dinners only, but a la carte appetizers and desserts are offered for added enjoyment in your dining experience.

Appetizers

DUNGENESS CRAB LEG COCKTAIL SUPREME – Oregon's finest.

OYSTER COCKTAIL SUPREME – Tiny Pacific or Kumamoto oysters.

OREGON SHRIMP COCKTAIL SUPREME – The flavorful ones.
Served with zesty red cocktail sauce and a splash of Sauterne wine.

ESCARGOTS A LA BOURGUIGNONNE – baked in their shells with garlic butter, served with warmed sourdough bread.

Desserts

CHEESECAKE – New York style, heavy, creamy and rich with cream cheese and eggs.

CASHEW - KUMQUAT PIE – An original you'll long remember.

CHIFFON OR CREAM PIES – Created in our kitchen, superbly unique.

BRANDIED FRUIT PARFAIT – The ultimate dessert: A seasonally changing melange of fresh fruit macerated in brandy and layered with vanilla ice cream, topped with whipped cream and rummy blueberries.

"FOOD WORTH WAITING FOR"

We are proud to present the finest quality seafoods, each item prepared to order in its own individual pan to preserve the delicate, distinctive flavor. To complement and amplify these flavors, we cook with fresh creamery butter only; nothing is battered or deep fried. Our kind of food preparation takes time; please be patient. You're our customer; you deserve the best.

Seafood Dinners

COQUILLES SAINT JACQUES — Tender scallops poached in white wine, tossed in a mushroom veloute sauce, and baked with a buttered crumb topping, sparked with Parmesan cheese.

PRAWNS — Jumbo prawns, butterflied, lightly dusted with fine cracker meal, and pan-fried in butter.

STUFFED CRAB CASSEROLE — Dungeness crabmeat, baked with water chestnuts, celery, sourdough breadcrumbs and herbs. A symphony of flavors and textures.

CRAB LEGS — Local Dungeness, of course, poached in a white wine bouillon, served with drawn butter.

* HALIBUT CHEEKS — A real gourmet treat. Wine-dipped, dusted with cracker meal, and sauteed in butter with fresh ginger root.

* OYSTERS — Choice, tiny Pacific or Kumamoto oysters, always fresh, always firm, summer or winter (from Newport's Yaquina Bay). Sauteed in butter.

* SCALLOPS — The sweetest fruit of the sea, briefly browned in butter and served at their tender, succulent best.

LITTLE NECK CLAMS — Steamed with white wine, celery and herbs. Served with rich nectar and drawn butter.

LOBSTER IN BLACK BEAN SAUCE — For a change of pace, we offer this oriental favorite. Slipper lobster meat, cooked in flavorful black bean sauce with scallions and garlic. Served with rice.

HALIBUT STEAK — A thick steak, marinated in white wine, dipped in seasoned flour, and pan-fried in butter with ginger root.

MOULES MARINIERE — Fresh mussels in a broth just begging to be dunked with crusty French bread.

Other entrees will be served depending upon season, availability, and the cook's disposition. Your waiter or waitress will inform you.

The Adobe

at
Yachats, Oregon

THE builders of The Adobe Resort/Motel took great care not to disturb the natural beauty of the countryside. The restaurant, an integral part of the facility, was designed to complement that beauty. It is alive with warm lights, stained glass, handmade adobe bricks, clusters of antiques, natural woods, beamed ceilings—all accenting and heightening the spells of the outdoors. Built at the ocean's edge, the wall of windows exposes a view of the surf pounding and thrashing upon the rugged rocks below. The Adobe has garnered the attention of such publications as Harper's and Sunset not only for this view but also for its cuisine. We're convinced you, too, will enjoy your encounter with this place of solitary beauty.

The Adobe
Highway 101, 1 mile north of Yachats
P.O. Box 219
Yachats, OR 97498

547-3141

Hours: Summer and Winter weekends
8-11 am breakfast, 6-9 pm dinner
Winter weekdays
8-10 am breakfast, 6-8 pm dinner
No holiday closures

Libations: Full wine list, cocktails, and beer

Payment: VISA, Mastercharge, and
personal checks

Reservations: Suggested

The Adobe
Crab Suzy

Lauren Smith's Crab Suzy calls for rolled standard French pancakes as a base, flaked crab meat as the filling, and a special "suzy" sauce.

Easy-Do French Pancakes

In a deep quart bowl, combine 2 eggs, 1 cup flour, 1 cup milk and ½ teaspoon salt. Beat thoroughly until smooth.

Fry individually in 6" cast iron frypan.

To do this, heat and thoroughly oil pan. Pour in 2 tablespoons batter; shake pan to distribute it to edge and make thin pancake. Turn when lightly browned.

The pancakes may be prepared ahead, covered with foil and refrigerated. Makes 10-12.

To Fill

Center each pancake with ¼ pound flaked crab meat. Roll up and press into neat long rolls. Bake in oiled individual long low casseroles that can go to table. Or, place the "suzy" rolls, fold-side-down, an inch apart, in oiled shallow pan. Pour over Suzy Sauce, being sure all exposed pancake surfaces are moistened to prevent scorching. Dust each roll with 2 heaping tablespoons coarse-shredded Cheddar cheese.

Bake in hot oven, 400°F., until cheese melts and sauce is bubbling hot.

Suzy Sauce

Combine, mix and heat together 6 ounce can tomato paste, 2 cups rich chicken stock and ⅓ dry white wine.

Serves 6.

Appetizers

All appetizers served with our cheese rolls

Shrimp Cocktail. . . . .

Shrimp Cocktail Supreme. . . . .

Crab Cocktail. . . . .

Crab Cocktail Supreme . . . .

Cup of Clam Chowder . . . .

Steamer Clams . . . .
Served in their shells with drawn butter.

Prawns . . . .
Fried to a golden brown, served with lemon and our own cocktail sauce

Dinner

Choice of Clam Nectar or Tomato Juice or Soup du Jour or Clam Chowder. Tossed Salad with choice of the Ado homemade dressings, Baked Potato, French Fires or Rice Pilaf, Toasted Cheese Roll — Plain Roll if you wish.

Seafood

Scallops. . . . .
Plump scallops, lightly breaded and fried to a golden brown

Giant Prawns. . . . .
French fried to a golden brown and served with our own tasty hot sauce

Fried Oysters . . . .
Petite tender oysters simmered delicately to a golden brown

Crab Suzy . . . .
AN ADOBE CHEF'S SPECIAL, tender, fresh crabmeat wrapped in a French pancake covered with a rich tomato sauce and melted cheese. This delightful dish is served bubbling hot from our oven

Australian Lobster Tail . . . One Tail / Two Tails
The finest Australian Lobster tails broiled and proudly served with drawn butter and lemon wedge

Crab Legs . . . .
Deep fried Dungeness Crab legs lightly breaded and deep fried to a golden brown

Lobster Thermadore. . . . .
Hearty pieces of lobster in a delicious sharp cheese and dry sauterne wine cream sauce

Pacific Halibut . . . .
Grilled, served with butter, our own tartar sauce and lemon wedge

Fried Razor Clams . . . .
Tender local clams fried to a golden brown in pure butter and lemon wedge

Steamed Butter Clams . . . .
Served in their shells with drawn butter and lemon wedge

The Adobe Seafood Platter. . . . . .
Clams, Prawns, Scallops, Oysters, Crab Leg, and Halibut with cocktail and tartar sauce and lemon wedge

Baked Fresh Salmon (In season). . . . . .
A hearty fillet served with cream sauce and lemon wedge

Boned Trout Almondine. . . . . . .
Large, firm mountain trout fried in butter and lemon wedge

Shrimp Orleans . . . .
Light baby shrimp under a rich creamy sauce that oozes butter. This is served with toast points

The Adobe Steak and Lobster
Australian lobster tail combined with a choice Filet prepared to your liking.

...her Entrees

Chicken. . . . .
Quality young honey-dipped chicken pieces fried golden brown

Lamb Chops . . . .
Two Large Loin, broiled to order, served with mint jelly

Special of the Day

(Please ask Waitress) . . . (Priced Daily)

...om Our Broiler

Served to you on a Sizzling Platter

...et Mignon. . . . .
10 oz., extra thick center cut of Filet, a real pleasure.

...ew York Cut Steak . . . .
12 oz., thick cut to be flavorful and juicy, broiled to your order

Choice Top Sirloin . . . .
12 oz. of choice top sirloin served the way you like it

Beef Tournedo . . . .
AN ADOBE CHEF'S SPECIAL, juicy Tenderloin with Broiled Tomato, Artichoke Bottoms, Bearnaise Sauce, Mushrooms, and choice of Potato

...ghter Choices

...ew England Clam Chowder . . . .
A generous pot of rich creamy chowder served with Crackers, Hearts of Lettuce, choice of Dressings, and Toasted Cheese Rolls

...ungeness Crab or
...rimp Louis. . . . . Shrimp
Crab
Combination
Our own Louis served with fresh garden greens, choice of dressing, and Toasted Cheese Rolls. A Real Delight

Small Fry

(12 and Under)
Includes French Fries, Milk or Soda, and Ice Cream

Chicken. . . . .
Giant Prawns. . . . .
Fish and Chips . . . .
Hamburger . . . .
Peanut Butter and
Jelly Sandwich . . . .

...everages

...offee, Tea . . . . Milk . . . . Soft Drinks . . . .

Our wine offers a complete selection of wines to enhance your dinner.
Finish your dining with our excellent Adobe House Drink:
"Misty Fog" —

...esserts

...omemade pies and cakes . . . .
...hocolate Eclairs . . . .
...undaes . . . .
...ruit Tarts . . . .
...e Cream . . . .

La Serre

LA Serre cultivates the feeling of a French country kitchen with its open cooking area, abundance of greenery, spotting of antiques, emphasis on natural woods, and a pervading, sparkling cleanliness. It's a relatively new restaurant on the scene with a character and flavor all its own: a crisp and uncompromising approach to the proper preparation of foods for discriminating diners. Owner Sylvia Towers takes particular pride in La Serre's being a special place for special people; it's an alternative eatery. There are no short cuts here; only the most natural ingredients are used. As Sylvia herself likes to put it: "Healthful foods because we care".

La Serre
2nd and Beach Street
Yachats, OR 97498

547-3420

Hours: Summer 9 am-10 pm Wed.-Mon.
Winter 5 pm- 9 pm Mon., Wed., Thurs.
9 am-10 pm weekends
Closed Christmas

Libations: Full wine list, cocktails, and beer

Payment: VISA, Mastercharge, and American Express

Reservations: Advised

La Serre
Avocado Lime Pie

Rich and to be served in small slices—the perfect summer dessert.

The Crust

1½ cups graham crackers, ground fine
1 cube butter, melted
grated nutmeg
touch of cinnamon

Mix this and press into pie pan. Put into preheated oven 350 °F. for 4 minutes. Remove from oven and let cool.

The Filling

3 very ripe avocados
½ cup cream
½ cup honey (more or less to taste and strength of honey)
8 ounces cream cheese at room temperature
1½ limes (squeeze juice)

In food processor blend avocados; slowly add cream, lime juice, honey—drop bits of cream cheese a little at a time. Put mixture into crust.

The Icing: an essential contrast to filling

8 ounces cream cheese
dash of honey
½ lime, juiced

Blend ingredients until smooth—carefully with rubber spatula smooth on top of filling. Refrigerate overnight before serving.

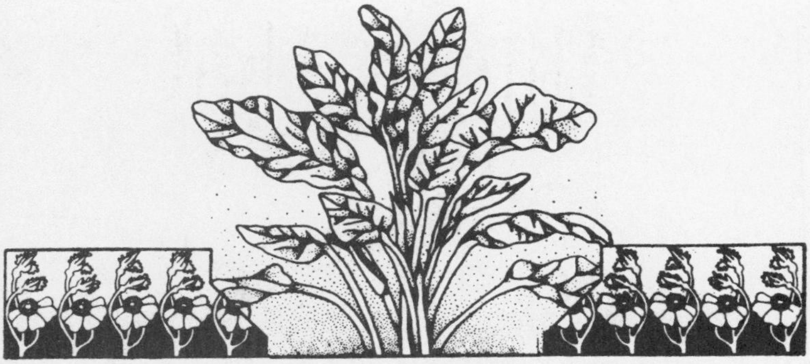

plates

Served with Homemade Soup or Green Salad, Fresh Vegetable,
Brown and Wild Rice or Steamed Red Potato, Fresh Baked Bread and Butter

Baked Cornish Game Hens *Whole* *Half*

Fresh Rockfish (In Season)

Seafarer Grill

Sautéed Oregon Razor Clams

Sautéed Yaquina Bay Oysters

Baked Chinook Salmon with Capers

Sautéed New Orleans Prawns

Baked Nova Scotia Scallops

Cioppino
Medley of Shellfish in a Tomato Vegetable Sauce

Top Sirloin Steak — Charbroiled

New York Steak — Charbroiled

Child's Portion (Under 12 Years)

soups & salads

Served with Fresh Baked Bread and Butter

Manhattan Clam Chowder *Bowl* *Cup*

Soup *Bowl* *Cup*

Vegetable Salad *Dinner Salad*

Shrimp Louie

this & that

Shrimp Cocktail

Mushrooms for Two
Sautéed in Butter, Wine and Herbs

Bowl of Fresh Fruit (In Season)

Savory Spinach Quiche
Served with Soup

Roast Beef Sandwich
Tomato, Fresh Mushrooms and Sprouts

Shrimp Sandwich
Oregon Shrimp and Melted Cheese, Garnished

French Dip
Served on French Roll with Au Jus and Salad

Vegetarian Sandwich
Avocado, Tomato, Fresh Mushrooms, Cheese and Sprouts

Steamed Red Potato
or
Brown and Wild Rice

desserts

Apple Strudel
Poppyseed Cake
Cheesecake
Sherbet
Ice Cream

beverages

Smoothies
Fresh Fruit Blended with Apple Juice

Tea.
Herb Tea
Columbian Coffee
Mineral Water
Natural Juices
Iced Teas
Milk
Cappucino
Espresso

PLEASE ASK YOUR WAITRESS ABOUT OUR SPECIALS

Beulah's Sea View Inn

Yachats, Oregon

THIS restaurant, started by Beulah herself over 40 years ago, originally seated 15 people. Now 150 patrons can dine in the charm of this family style restaurant, where the atmosphere is casual and informal. Every table has a bird's eye view of Yachats Bay and the densely timbered lands. Owners Richard Heath and Larry Zimmerman pride themselves on "good home cooking" woven into a number of innovative dishes. Their reputation is nationwide, even capturing the acclaim of gourmet James Beard. But Beulah's real fame rests principally on the pride with which they welcome and please the individual diner—as you can deliciously discover for yourself.

Beulah's Sea View Inn
Highway 101 West
P.O. Box 175
Yachats, OR 97498

547-3215

Hours: 11 am-10 pm Thurs.-Tues.
Closed Wed. Also closed Jan. 1-Feb. 9

Libations: Full wine list, cocktails, and beer

Payment: Personal checks

Reservations: Suggested

Beulah's Sea View Inn Gourmet Scalloped Oysters

4-6 tablespoons Tillamook yearling oysters
approximately ¾ cup milk
2 tablespoons chopped onion
2 tablespoons butter
2 shakes of season all salt
buttered croutons
dash of garlic powder (optional)

Place oysters in buttered individual oven casserole dish. Add milk, onion, butter and salt. Top with croutons. Bake at 425°F. until croutons are golden brown. Serves 1.

A Treat You Won't Forget

CHEF'S SEAFOOD PLATTER

Prawns, Scallops, Crab Legs,
Oysters, Clams, Halibut,
Salmon and Fish Cutlets
All this and more
Soup – Salad – Bran Muffins,
Coffee or Tea

Beulah's Famous Old-Fashioned

CHICKEN AND DUMPLINGS

Served with Soup and Salad

Kitchen Fresh Bran Muffins

Southern Style Corn Fritters

Coffee or Tea

SEAFOOD COCKTAIL

CRAB MEAT COCKTAIL . . . . .

SHRIMP COCKTAIL . . . .

OYSTER COCKTAIL . . . .

Served with Salted Wafers and Coffee

SOUPS

CLAM CHOWDER. . . . .

OYSTER STEW. . . . .

SOUP DU JOUR . . . .

Served with Salted Wafers and Coffee

TASTY-FRESH SALAD

MIXED GREEN with CRAB MEAT .

MIXED GREEN with SHRIMP . . .

CRAB LOUIS . . . .

SHRIMP LOUIS . . . .

MOLDED SALAD . . . .

DINNER SALAD . . . .

Served with Bran Muffins and Coffee

BEVERAGES

COFFEE. . . . .

TEA Hot or Ice . . . .

SANKA . . . .

MILK . . Small . . Large . .

POP. . . . .

OCEAN FRESH SEAFOOD DINNERS

All dinners below are served with Soup & Salad, Our Kitchen Fresh Bran Muffins, (Beulah's Tomato Preserves), Southern Style Corn Fritters.
Coffee or Tea

PRAWNS. . . . .

FISH and CHIPS . . . .

SCALLOPS . . . .

OYSTERS . . . .

RAZOR CLAMS . . . .

FILLET of SOLE . . . .

FRESH HALIBUT . . . .

FRESH SALMON . . . .

DINNERS FOR CHILDREN

(Under 10 years of age)
Ground Beef Patty, French-Fried or Mashed Potatoes, Jello-Fruit Salad, Muffins.
Milk and Dessert

CHICKEN and DUMPLINGS . . .

FISH and CHIPS. . . . .

SCALLOPS . . . .

ROAST BEEF. . . . .

BAKED HAM . . . .

Served with same as above

SIDE ORDERS

BAKED POTATO. . . . .

FRENCH FRIES. . . . .

CUP OF CHOWDER . . . .

2 BRAN MUFFINS. . . . .
WITH BUTTER, TOMATO PRESERVES AND COFFEE

CORN FRITTERS . . . .
SIDE OF TWO

OTHER DINNER SUGGESTIONS

All dinners below are served with Soup & Salad, our Kitchen Fresh Bran Muffins, (Beulah's Tomato Preserves), Southern Style Corn Fritters Coffee or Tea

PENCER STEAK . . . .
with Baked Potato

IUSHROOM STEAK . . . . . .
with Mashed Potatoes

PECIAL STEAK . . . .
with Baked Potato

OAST BEEF . . . .
and Horse Radish if requested

AMBURGER STEAK . . . . . .
Grilled Onions if requested

HICKEN FRIED STEAK . . . .
with Mashed Potatoes

AKED HAM . . . .
Beulah's Mustard Sauce

AKED PORK CHOP . . . . . .
with Dressing

SOUTHERN FRIED CHICKEN .

8-INCH RAINBOW TROUT . . .
Choice of Whipped or French Fried Potato

ROASTED OREGON TURKEY .
With all the Trimmings

CHICKEN ALA WALDORF . . .
Served on a French Puff Pastrie

CRAB CASSEROLE . . . . . .
Crab in a Red and Green Pepper Sauce

CRAB LEGS AU GRATIN . . .
Smooth and Mild Cheese Sauce

LOBSTER THERMIDOR . . . .
Cubed Lobster Meat Sauteed with Mushrooms and Sherry Wine, Sprinkled with Parmesan Cheese, topped with Buttered Crumbs

SPECIALTIES OF THE CHEF

Complete Dinners

OCEAN FRESH
EA FOOD CASSEROLE

A Wonderful Casserole Dish
Five kinds of Seafood
In a Delicious Sauce
A Real Treat!

GOURMET SCALLOPED
OYSTERS

Fresh Oysters from Tillamook, Oregon are used in this dish. A Gourmet's Delight.

OYSTER ST. CHARLES

Oysters Sauteed in butter, then placed in a Red and Green Pepper sauce. You will be back for this one.

SANDWICHES

TEAK SANDWICH . . . . . .

RAB SANDWICH . . . .
Soup — Salad — Coffee

AMBURGER. . . . .

AMBURGER with FRENCH FRIES

CHEESEBURGER . . . .

CHEESEBURGER
with FRENCH FRIES . . .

Served with
Tomatoes - Onions - Pickles
Beulah's Hamburger Relish
and Coffee

DESSERTS

EULAH'S SPECIAL — CUSTARD BREAD PUDDING topped with Whipping Cream . . .

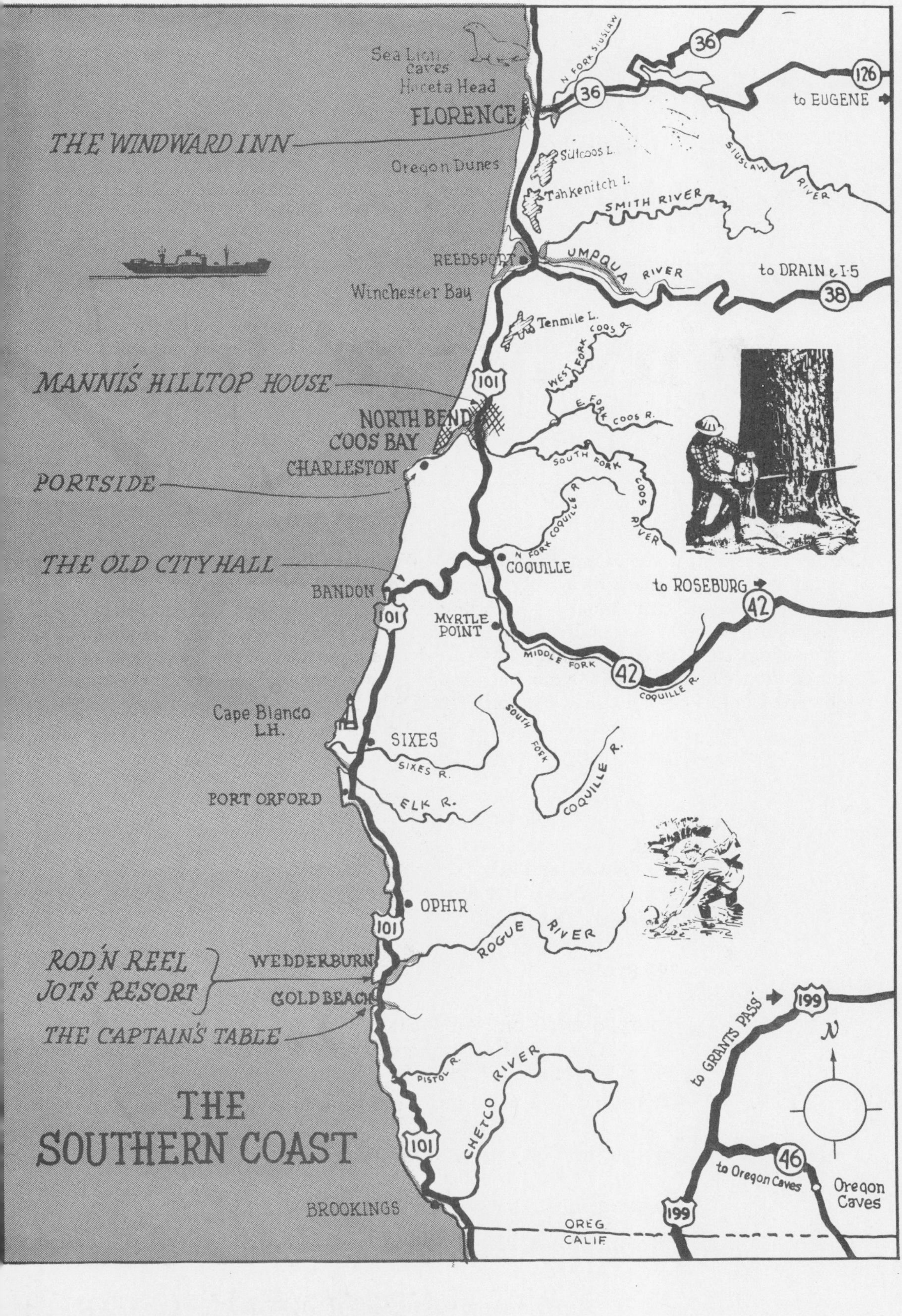
THE SOUTHERN COAST
THE WINDWARD INN
MANNI'S HILLTOP HOUSE
PORTSIDE
THE OLD CITY HALL
ROD'N REEL
JOT'S RESORT
THE CAPTAIN'S TABLE
Sea Lion Caves
Heceta Head
FLORENCE
Oregon Dunes
Siltcoos L.
Tahkenitch L.
SMITH RIVER
SIUSLAW RIVER
N FORK SIUSLAW
to EUGENE
REEDSPORT
UMPQUA RIVER
Winchester Bay
to DRAIN & I-5
Tenmile L.
WEST FORK COOS R.
E FORK COOS R.
SOUTH FORK COOS RIVER
N FORK COQUILLE R.
NORTH BEND
COOS BAY
CHARLESTON
COQUILLE
BANDON
to ROSEBURG
MYRTLE POINT
MIDDLE FORK COQUILLE R.
SOUTH FORK
COQUILLE R.
Cape Blanco L.H.
SIXES
SIXES R.
PORT ORFORD
ELK R.
OPHIR
ROGUE RIVER
WEDDERBURN
GOLD BEACH
PISTOL R.
CHETCO RIVER
to GRANTS PASS
to Oregon Caves
Oregon Caves
BROOKINGS
OREG.
CALIF.
N
36
126
38
101
42
199
46

Windward Inn

BORN as a gas station and lunch counter, The Windward Inn has grown in increments until today it is the hallmark of a truly fine restaurant. Its stylish decor is rich in natural woods and alive with traditional yet sparkling architecture. Owners Van and Kathie Heeter are justifiably proud of the candlelit ambience of the Maxwell Room, the gift nook and package wine shop, the atmosphere of attentive service, and most of all the simply yet elegantly prepared food. Surely one of the most consistently excellent restaurants on the coast, The Windward Inn has been honored by Ford Times and other publications. Don't miss it!

The Windward Inn
3757 Highway 101 North
Florence, OR 97439

997-8243

Hours: 8 am-9 pm Tues.-Sun.
Closed Thanksgiving and Christmas

Libations: Full wine list, cocktails and beer

Payment: VISA and Mastercharge

Reservations: Only for private parties and large groups

The Windward Inn

Gratineéd Onion Soup

12 medium sweet onions (about 1½ pounds), thinly sliced
¼ cup oil
2 tablespoons butter
½ teaspoon sugar

In large pan melt butter with oil and add onions and sugar. Simmer slowly for at least one hour, stirring as needed. Onions should be rich, golden brown.

3 tablespoons flour
2 quarts stock or bouillon
(can be beef or half chicken/half beef)
½ cup dry sherry
½ teaspoon Dijon mustard
salt and pepper to taste

Sprinkle flour over onions and blend well. Turn off the heat, blend in the boiling stock or bouillon, then the sherry and mustard. Cover partially and simmer again on low heat for approximately 30-40 minutes. Season with pepper and salt to taste. Thin soup if necessary with additional stock or bouillon. Serves 8-12.

French bread slices one inch thick
butter
grated Swiss cheese
3 tablespoons brandy or cognac

Stir the brandy into the soup. Butter the French bread. Toast under the broiler. Ladle soup into heat-proof bowls, float the bread crouton on top and top that with the grated Swiss cheese. Run under the broiler until bubbly.

MISCELLANEA

APPETIZERS & SALADS

FRENCH ONION SOUP (substitution for dinner soup - extra) ....
FRESHLY SHUCKED RAW PETITE OYSTERS (minimum 3) .... each
PATE' MAISON (Home Made Liver Pate') ....
CRACKED DUNGENESS CRAB served on ice ....
OREGON SHRIMP COCKTAIL ....
LARGE DUNGENESS CRAB SALAD ....
LARGE OREGON SHRIMP SALAD ....
FRESH FRUIT SALAD PLATE with ice cream or sherbet ....
LARGE CHOPPED FRESH VEGETABLE SALAD (Small) ....
Fresh vegetables of the season, crisp romaine, vinaigrette dressing.
FRESH MUSHROOM SALAD with vinaigrette dressing (substitution for dinner salad - extra) ....

ACCOMPANIMENTS & EXTRA PORTIONS

COLE SLAW ....
FRENCH FRIED POTATOES ..
SARATOGA CHIPS ....
(Deep fried potato slices)
JELLO ....
STEAMED REDSKIN POTATO .....
BAKED POTATO ....
SMALL TOSSED GREEN SALAD ...
COTTAGE CHEESE ....
FRESH VEGETABLE OF THE DAY ..
FRESH SAUTEED MUSHROOMS ....

HOME MADE CONFECTIONS & DESSERTS

HOME MADE LAYER CAKE (a la Mode) ....
HOME MADE CHEESE CAKE ....
HOME MADE PIE (a la Mode) ....
FRESH FRUIT CREAM PIE WITH WHIPPED CREAM (in season) ....
WALNUT PIE (a la Mode) ....
ICE CREAM ....
CHOCOLATE ICE CREAM SUNDAE WITH WHIPPED CREAM AND NUTS ......
SHERBET ....
OTHER SPECIAL PASTRY OF THE DAY
(ask to see our pastry tray -- prices vary)

BEVERAGES

COFFEE (every pot ground fresh) ....
MILK or BUTTERMILK
POT of TEA ....
SOFT DRINKS ....
DECAFFEINATED COFFEE ....
HOT CHOCOLATE ....
ICED TEA ....

Bottled Beers - - - - Variously Priced
Cocktail Service Available in Dining Rooms After 4:30 PM

ENTRÉES

Please consult
our Wine List for suggestions to
complement your meal . . . We are pleased
to offer one of the most complete Wine Cellars in the State.

Entrées accompanied by home made soup, choice of salad (tossed green, cole slaw, jello or cottage cheese), potato, rice pilaf or fresh vegetable and home baked bread [Beverage extra]

STEAK & MEAT

(Our steaks are cut very thick and cooking them well done has a tendency to destroy flavor and tenderness.)

CHOICE TOP SIRLOIN STEAK .... 12 oz. 8 oz.
Selected choice western beef, thick and juicy. Broiled to your order.

CHOICE NEW YORK CUT STEAK (12 oz.) ....
Thick cut to be juicy and flavorful. Broiled to your order.

TERIYAKI STEAK ....
A choice small sirloin seasoned with our teriyaki marinade and sizzled on the Char-Broiler.

STEAK DIANE ....
A small sirloin -- pan sauteed in butter and accompanied by a wine and mushroom sauce made from the buttery concentrated essence of the pan drippings.

CHUCKWAGON STEAK (1/2 lb. lean ground beef) ....

VEAL CUTLETS (2) ....
Wisconsin Veal Slices dipped in seasoned bread crumbs and sauteed.

FRIED CHICKEN ....
Half of a fresh fryer, cooked to order. Please allow twenty minutes.

CHAR-BROILED CENTER CUT LAMB CHOPS ....
Lightly marinated with honey, brandy and marjoram and sizzled on the broiler. Chutney sauce.

"We drank the wine and ate the meat . . . We dined at the Inn that night in quiet contemplation of the fireglow . . ."

ENTRÉES

Please consult
our Wine List for suggestions to
complement your meal . . . We are pleased
to offer one of the most complete Wine Cellars in the State.

Entrées accompanied by home made soup, choice of salad (tossed green, cole slaw, jello or cottage cheese), potato, rice pilaf or fresh vegetable and home baked bread [Beverage extra]

SEAFOOD

OCEAN FISH CUTLETS ....
White Ling Cod from local coastal waters. Deep fried.

DEEP FRIED PRAWNS (6) in our own batter ....

PACIFIC HALIBUT STEAK grilled, broiled or poached ....

LOCAL RAZOR CLAMS from our grill ....

THE CAPTAIN'S BEST ....
Delicious seafood assortment. May vary with season and availability.

PACIFIC SALMON STEAK grilled, broiled, or poached ....

FILET OF PETRALE SOLE MEUNIERE ....
Fresh from local coastal waters, pan sauteed and served with nut brown butter.

BAKED YEARLING OYSTERS when available ....
These small, plump oysters are mild and sweet. Baked in their own shells and served with drawn butter. We recommend our Saratoga Chips (deep fried potato slices) with this entree.

FRESH CRACKED DUNGENESS CRAB, in season ....
Hot from the steamer with drawn butter or chilled on cracked ice.

BROILED TIGER PRAWNS ....
Large shrimp. Prepared like lobster with white wine and served with drawn butter.

LOBSTER TAIL 1 large. Served with drawn butter ....
Lobster/Sirloin Steak Combination ....

FRESH LOCAL OYSTERS from our grill ....

STEAMED LITTLENECK CLAMS ....
"Butter" clams from local beaches hot from our steamer in a delicious broth. Served with drawn butter.

SEA MUSSELS MARINIERE (Not available July and August) ....
Steamed in a delicious broth of white wine, butter, onion and garlic. Perhaps our most abundant native shellfish, Mussels are seldom harvested commercially. To insure freshness, we gather our own from local beaches.

"The design of the sea is balance, its lesson . . . infinite patience, its gift . . . abundant harvest . . ."

LIGHTER FARE

We are happy to accommodate special dietary requests.

HOME MADE SOUP OF THE DAY (except chowder) .... Tureen ....
Small Bowl ......

HOME MADE CLAM CHOWDER .... Tureen ....
Small Bowl ......

THE SOUP DEAL (with chowder ....
Large tureen of home made soup, a chunk of cheese, fresh fruit and a poppin' fresh roll from our bakery.

CLAM BASKET ....
Deep fried tender, sweet clam strips served with French fries, cole slaw or salad and hot roll.

STEAK SANDWICH ....
6 oz. Sirloin steak, French fries, toast and green salad.

MANHATTAN ....
Home made Pate' (ground chicken liver, beef, pork and seasoning), toasted Bagel or special bread, fresh fruit, and a small bowl of today's soup.

FISH 'N' CHIPS ....
Served with choice o f cole slaw or salad and hot roll.

V.I.P PLATE

(for Juniors or Seniors)

BROILED GROUND BEEF ....
CRISPY FRIED FISH CUTLET ..
ROAST TOM TURKEY ....

Served with steamed redskin potatoes, Jello, toast and jelly.
French fries extra

WELCOME FAMILIES!

Although we do serve alcoholic beverages, it is our intent to provide a comfortable family dining atmosphere. Children are always welcome at the Windward Inn.

SANDWICHES

CHEESE SANDWICH, grilled or plain (Swiss) ....

THE ORIGINAL AMERICAN HAMBURGER

OUR WAY ....
A big, juicy hamburger, special sesame bun, mayonnaise, lettuce, tomato, onion and pickle.

STANDARD SIZE ....
Small burger, same trimmings.

Add CHEESE ....

Add FRENCH FRIES ....

MANNI'S HILLTOP HOUSE

MANNI'S Hilltop House perches high above Coos Bay, revealing an impressive vista of water and Oregon dunes. Heavy ship traffic from the busy port plys the bay waters and local fishing boats dot the horizon. Owner Manni Wieseke has brought with him to this endeavor a rich and proud German heritage. It is this combination of European hospitality, the agreeable surroundings, impeccable service and expansive menu which enhances the dining pleasure, and indicates a quality restaurant catering to a particular patronage. We know Manni's Hilltop House will be high on your list of favorite places on the southern coast.

Manni's Hilltop House
166 North Bay Drive
North Bend, OR 97459

756-6515

Hours: Dinner 5-11 pm Mon.-Sat., 5-9 pm Sun.
Brunch 10 am-2 pm Sun.
No holiday closures

Libations: Full wine list, cocktails, and beer

Payment: VISA, Mastercharge,
American Express, and
Carte Blanche

Reservations: Suggested

Manni's Hilltop House Pepper Steak

1 New York steak, 12-14 ounces
2 tablespoons crushed peppercorns
1 cup basic brown sauce
½ cup sliced mushrooms
¼ cup Burgundy wine
salt, MSG, garlic to taste

Sauté mushrooms in butter, add brown sauce and Burgundy. Pat the peppercorns onto the steak, season with MSG, salt and pepper and broil to taste. Top the steak with sauce when it is ready. Serves 1.

APPETIZERS

SHRIMP COCKTAIL Supreme

SHRIMP COCKTAIL Dinner Size

DUNGENESS CRAB COCKTAIL Supreme

DUNGENESS CRAB COCKTAIL Dinner Size

TUREEN OF BUTTER CLAMS

SIX OYSTERS ON THE HALF SHELL

ESCARGOT BOURGIGNON

CLAM NECTAR

SOUPS AND SALADS

BOSTON CLAM CHOWDER Tureen
Cup

CRAB LOUIS

SHRIMP LOUIS

BOUILLABAISSE

Our Specialty

A tureen of shrimp, crab legs, butter clams, red snapper, scallops, halibut and prawns. Delicately simmered in our own secret wine and herb broth. Served with tossed green salad and garlic bread. We add a tidy bib.

Our dinners are served with choice of Boston clam chowder or tossed green salad, a baked potato, french fries or rice pilaf and garlic bread or rolls.

Chef Hans Steiner's international veal dishes are prepared from the finest fresh, milk fed veal from Wisconsin. An extra large portion is available, please ask your server.

VEAL PICCATA MILANAISE (Italy) Slices of tenderloin veal dipped in eggs and parmesan cheese. Sauteed and topped with fresh mushrooms.

VEAL CORDON BLEU (Switzerland)
Veal stuffed with ham and swiss cheese.

WIENER SCHNITZEL (Austria)
An old Vienna favorite. Thinly sliced veal breaded and pan fried.

VEAL OSCAR (France)
A tender veal steak topped with asparagus spears, crab meat and hollandaise sauce.

GREAT COMBINATIONS

OUR FAMOUS SALESMAN'S SIRLOIN (the original) An 8 oz. U.S.D.A. choice steak wrapped in bacon and broiled with tender care, large dungeness crab legs topped with a nippy cheddar cheese sauce. Served with a wedge of lemon and a mushroom.

SURF AND TURF
A succulent combination of broiled rock lobster tail and a choice cut of filet mignon, served with lemon butter and french fried onion rings.

BEEF AND REEF A combination of a choice top sirloin and deep fried scampi; served with red sauce and a lemon wedge.

And how about an order of fresh sauteed mushrooms? or asparagus spears with hollandaise sauce?

SEAFOOD DINNERS

BROILED FILET OF CHINOOK SALMON

When in Season Please ask your server

Fresh from the waters of the Pacific Ocean. Served with a lemon wedge.

FRENCH FRIED PRAWNS

Large prawns from the Gulf of Mexico, served with cocktail sauce.

DEEP FRIED DUNGENESS CRAB LEGS

When available

Coos Bay's famous delicacy, utterly delicious flavor, served with cocktail sauce.

CRAB ALA NEWBURG

Glazed with sharp cheddar cheese and served with toast points en casserole.

ABALONE STEAK AMANDINI

From the Gulf of Lower California. With lemon wedge, both tartar and cocktail sauce.

GRILLED FRESH PACIFIC OYSTERS

Lemon wedge, tartar sauce.

OYSTERS BURGUNDY

Tender, petite Pacific oysters, slowly baked in the shell over rock salt in a burgundy wine sauce.

GRILLED NORTHERN HALIBUT STEAK

The king of white fish, served with lemon wedge and tartar sauce.

NEW ENGLAND SEA SCALLOPS

Tender sea scallops deep fried to a golden brown. Served with lemon wedge; tartar and red sauce.

STUFFED FILET OF ENGLISH SOLE

Filled with a shrimp and rice stuffing.

GRILLED SEASIDE RAZOR CLAMS

Tartar sauce, lemon wedge.

BROILED AUSTRALIAN ROCK LOBSTER TAILS

Prepared in the shell. Served with drawn lemon butter.

FRESH FILLET OF SOLE

Grilled, served with tartar sauce.

BROILED SCAMPI

Carefully broiled in wine and butter. Served with drawn butter and wedge of lemon.

HILLTOP SPECIALTIES

FRESH STEAMED BUTTER CLAMS

Served with melted lemon butter, a tossed salad and garlic bread

CAPTAIN'S SEAFOOD PLATTER

A choice selection of delicious halibut, salmon, oyster, prawns, scallops, crab legs, razor clams and sauces.

LOBSTER THERMIDORE

Prepared in a rich cardinal sauce. Seasoned with wine, herbs and mushrooms, and topped with sharp cheddar cheese. Served on the half shell.

LONG ISLAND ROAST DUCKLING ESPAGNOL

Served with green onions, bell peppers, olives and tomatoes sauteed in white wine, garnished with cherries and mandarin oranges.

BROILED STEAK DINNERS

NEW YORK CUT Boneless sirloin strip of U.S.D.A. choice beef. 16 oz.
12 oz.

HILLTOP PEPPER STEAK 12 oz. center cut
New York prepared with Madeira sauce, Peppercorns, Sherry wine and brown mushroom sauce.

FILET MIGNON A superb Steak. 12 oz.
8 oz.

TOP SIRLOIN STEAK 12 oz.
Very juicy, fine flavored beef, served on a sizzling platter. 8 oz.
6 oz.

ROAST PRIME RIB OF BEEF, au jus one a logger would love
generous portion

BROILED CHOPPED SIRLOIN OF PRIME BEEF
We prepare our own. Served in fresh mushroom gravy.

BROCHETTE OF BEEF
Tender tips of choice beef broiled on a sword with mushrooms, green peppers and onions. Served on a bed of rice pilaf with broiled tomato.

TORNEDOS OF BEEF With Choron sauce.

BEEF MEDALLION A delicacy prepared with Champagne sauce, slices of mushroom and choice Tenderloin.

FOR OUR YOUNG FRIENDS AND THE NOT SO HUNGRY FOLKS

BOUNTIFUL CHEESEBURGER WITH FRIES

FRENCH DIP SANDWICH

THE FINAL TOUCH

ICE CREAM **ICE CREAM SUNDAES**

CHEESECAKE

LOCATED on placid Charleston harbor, looking out over the boat basin and tidal flats prolific with clams, Portside is the newest addition to the Coos Bay area's list of fine restaurants, and is among the very best anywhere on the coast. The interior is contemporary but warm, with vaulted ceilings and a light and airy feeling. You'll be impressed with the diversity of choices on the menu, with many items accompanied by their own fragrant sauces, revealing the slow and careful attention needed for creation. If you're partial to seafood, it will be well worth the effort of negotiating your way to Portside.

Portside
Charleston Avenue & Wasson Street
Charleston, OR 97420

888-5544

Hours: 11 am-11 pm daily

Libations: Full wine list, cocktails, and beer

Payment: VISA, Mastercharge, and American Express

Reservations: Strongly recommended

Portside

Civet De Canard (Duck)

1 4-pound duck
½ pound chopped onion
16 ounces sliced mushrooms
2 shallots
½ pint Chambertin red wine
2 cups heavy cream
½ pound chopped bacon
bay leaf
thyme
coriander
whole black pepper

Cut the duck into ten pieces and sauté in oil and butter, strain the grease when the pieces are golden brown. Add the mushrooms, onion, bacon, chopped shallots, diced duck liver, and sauté for five minutes. Add red wine, bay leaf, thyme, whole black pepper and a touch of coriander. Simmer for 30 minutes. Remove duck and add cream to sauce. Reduce the sauce until thick, constantly stirring. Allow forty minutes for cooking. Serves 6. (Don't worry about the redness around the bones, this is the way duck should be eaten.)

Welcome . . .

to the Portside at Charleston. We are happy to see you and will strive to show you a memorable evening.

Our chef, Thierry Adam, came to the Oregon Coast via San Francisco from his native region of Bretagne, located on the northern coast of France.

We hope you will enjoy Thierry's touch and the menu that offers new experiences and tastes.

Hors d'Oeuvres/Appetizers

SHRIMP COCKTAIL — Dinner / Supreme

DUNGENESS CRAB COCKTAIL — Dinner / Supreme

SIX OYSTERS ON THE HALF SHELL

ÉSCARGOTS

STEAMED CLAMS

SMOKED SALMON ON RYE

PATÉ MAISON, a delicate cold cut

JAMBON CRU, ham wrapped in melon slice

Potages / Soups

SOUP DU JOUR

CLAM CHOWDER

BISQUE DE POISSON
Fish Bisque

SOUP A L'OIGNON GRATINÉE
French Onion Soup Au Gratin

Our dinners are served with choice of soup du jour or our green salad with choice of dressing. We recommend our house dressing.

Poissons / Fish

TRUITE POCHÉE SAUCE AURORE
Poached trout with cream saffron sauce and shrimp meat

FILET DE SAUMON SAUCE CARDINAL
Filet of Salmon with sauce cardinal

DÁRNE DE SAUMON—GRILLÉ A L'ANIS
Broiled Salmon with anise sauce

SCAMPI A L'ARMAGNAC
Scampi served with challots, flamed with Armagnac

PRAWNS PROVENCALE
Prawns sauteed in garlic butter, tomato and white wine

PRAWNS — Deep Fried to a Golden Brown
Served with lemon wedge, red and tartar sauce

FILET DE HALIBUT SAUCE DIÉPPOISE
Filet of Halibut with a cream sauce made of shrimp, mushrooms, challots and a touch of garlic

FILET DE SOLE GUÉRIM
Poached Filet of Sole served on cream of spinach

FILET DE SOLE VÉRONIQUE
Poached Filet of Sole served with noodles, nutmeg cream sauce and grape

REX SOLE SAUTÉE AMANDINE
Sauteed Rex Sole with almonds, butter and lemon

DOVER SOLE AU BEURRE D'AMCHOIX (imported)
Sauteed and served with a creamy anchovie butter

LA COQUILLE ST. JACQUES — PERSILLÉE
Scallops sauteed with mushrooms, parsley, garlic, challots, brandy and cream

LA PALOURDE MARIMIERE
Steamed clams with white wine, cream, parsley, garlic and challots

LA QUEUE DE LANGOUSTE AU GRATIN
Sliced lobstertail with saffron sauce and grated cheese

LE RED SNAPPER AUX CAPRES
Poached Red Snapper with creamy mustard and caper sauce

Viandes / Meats

LA BROCHETTE D'AGMEAU ALA MENTHE
Brochette of Lamb served with menthe sauce

LA COTE D'AGMEAU VERT PRÉS
Lamb chops with Tarragon sauce

LE STEAK AU POIVRE VERT
A New York Steak sauteed with green pepper corns, brandy, mustard, brown sauce and cream

LE ROTI DE BOEUF AU JUS
Prime Rib of Beef

LE TOURNEDOS RICHELIEU
Two large medallions of Filet Mignon served with artichoke, mushrooms and sherry wine sauce

NEW YORK—12 ounce, U.S.D.A.

FILET MIGNON—12 ounce, U.S.D.A.

Specialitees/Specialties

BOUILLABAISE MARSEILLAISE

BROCHETTE DE FRUIT
DE MER BEARNAISE SAUCE
Seafood brochette with bearnaise sauce

LE VEAU ST. JACQUES
Medallion of veal sauteed with scallops,
mushrooms, brandy, cream and paprika

RIS DE VEAU AUX OLIVES
Sweetbread sauteed with mushrooms,
black olives and sherry wine

LE PIGEON AUX MANDARINES
One roast pidgeon stuffed with wild rice,
liver and served with mandarine sauce

Desserts

PEACH MELBA
Peach, vanilla ice cream, melba sauce and whipped cream

POIRE BELLE HELENE
Pear on vanilla ice cream,chocolate,
whipped cream and toasted almonds

FRAISE DE PLOUGASTEL
Poached strawberries in Grand Marnier
on vanilla ice cream with whipped cream

PARFAIT MOKA

COUP "OLD CROW"
Vanilla ice cream with a shot of Old Crow chocolate
and whipped cream

HOMEMADE CHEESECAKE

HOMEMADE TART

CHOCOLATE MOUSSE

CRÉME CARAMEL

The Old City Hall

THIS old white structure, with its bell tower and shuttered windows, commands the attention of all who drive through Bandon. Its history is long, originally housing not only the City Hall but courtroom, fire department and library as well. Dan and Pam Thomas have remodeled it into a primary entertainment center for the Bandon area. The decor and atmosphere are strictly West Coast—airy, rough wood and verdant greenery. The bill of fare emphasizes local products. While The Old City Hall may have lost its municipal trappings, it has gained an uptempo beat that makes it great for food and merriment.

The Old City Hall
Filmore & 2nd on Highway 101
P.O. Box 763
Bandon, OR 97411

347-2763

Hours: Summer 11:30 am-9 pm daily
Winter 11:30 am-8 pm daily
Lounge 11:30 am-2:30 am daily
Closed Thanksgiving, Christmas, and New Year's Day

Libations: Wine, beer and cocktails

Payment: No credit cards—cash only

Reservations: Suggested in summer

The Old City Hall
Fresh Fish Chowder

2-3 pounds of fresh ling cod or red snapper
3 medium yellow onions, diced
¼ cup butter
10-12 medium potatoes
4 cans (13 ounces) condensed milk
salt, pepper and ground oregano to taste

Peel and dice potatoes to desired size and place in boiling, slightly salted water. Water should just cover the potatoes. Remove from heat as soon as tender. If you are dealing with whole fillets, remove the bones and then cut up into bite-sized pieces.

As soon as you remove potatoes from the heat, place cut up fish into your potato pot. This will poach fish and keep it very tender.

Place lid on pot and let set until ready to add the rest of the ingredients. In a saucepan place butter and when melted add diced onions. Cook until clear.

After you check to make sure fish is completely cooked, add onions, spices and milk. Serve hot. Makes 1 gallon.

If you wish to reheat chowder, be careful not to bring to boil or leave at too hot a temperature for a long period of time, or the milk will curdle.

Appetizers

Sliced Smoked Salmon ....

Shrimp Cocktail ..... Crab Cocktail .....

World's finest shellfish swimming in a rich cocktail sauce.

Homemade Onion Rings ....

Our specialty.

Raw Oysters ....

Half dozen local Charleston Oysters served with cocktail sauce, lemon wedges.

Sauteed Fresh Mushrooms ....

Large mushrooms, quartered and sauteed in garlic butter and herbs.

Fresh Fish Chowder ....

Deliciously fresh and served in a rich milk broth.

Steamed Clams, Chablis ....

One dozen Clams steamed in Chablis wine, served with lots of butter and lemon.

Fish and Shellfish

Fresh Charleston Oysters ....

Lightly breaded and fried to a golden brown.

Dungeness Crab - Whole ..... Half .....

Enjoy Crab the way the natives do, in the shell. Served with warm butter, rich cocktail sauce and tartar sauce.

Fish and Chips ....

Local and fresh, served golden brown with homemade french fries or baked potato.

Child's Fish and Chips ....

Just right for the small appetite of any age. Choice of baked potato or french fries.

Salmon Monique ....

Sauteed with fresh mushrooms and herbs.

Fresh Ling Cod Steak (when available) .....

A very tender and flaky fish that is grilled to a golden brown.

Fantail Shrimp ....

Half a dozen golden brown shrimp.

Razor Clams ....

For a real taste treat we lightly bread and quickly fry.

Scallops ....

Half a dozen fried to a golden brown.

Combination Seafood Platter ....

Fresh fish, Oysters, Scallops, Shrimp, Razor Clam.

Dinners above are served with cole slaw, warm garlic bread and baked potato with butter and sour cream unless we specify french fries. Please no substitutions.

Beefeaters

Steak and Crab ....

Fresh half Dungeness Crab, choice 5½ oz. Sirloin steak.

New York Steak (10-11 oz.) ....

Sirloin Steak (10-11 oz.) ....

Petite Sirloin (5½ oz.) ....

Filet Mignon (approx. 11 oz.) ....

Petite Filet Mignon (approx. 6 oz.) ....

Above dinners include homemade soup, toss green salad, baked potato with butter and sour cream and warm garlic bread.

Seafood Sandwiches

Fresh Crab Sandwich (in season) ....

Fresh Oyster Sandwich (in season) ....

Fresh Shrimp Sandwich (in season) ....

Salads

Chef's Seafood Salad Platter ....

Combination of Crab and Shrimp. Served with our own seafood dressing, sliced hard boiled egg and tomato wedges, garni.

Chef's Salad - Small ...... Large ......

Crab Louis ....

Shrimp Louis ....

A La Carte

Homemade French Fries ....

Baked Potato ....

Garlic Bread ....

Toss Green Salad ....

Beverages

Milk .... Tea .... Coffee .... Soft Drinks ....

Cocktails

ROD'n REEL

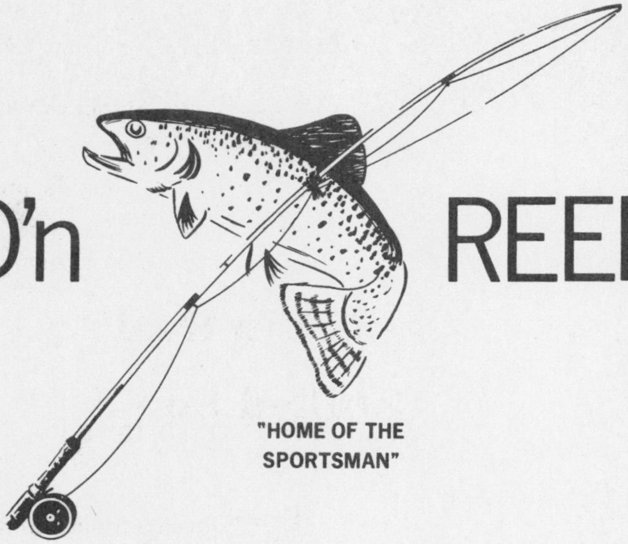

"HOME OF THE SPORTSMAN"

"YOU'RE a stranger here but once" declares the Rod 'n Reel's motto—and with good reason. It's a wonderfully cozy, friendly and comfortable place. It would seem as if the entire Powers family is involved in and committed to the enterprise of making your evening something special. Located on the bay of the mighty Rogue River, the Rod 'n Reel blends its congenial atmosphere with a fine view. The menu does not disappoint; a large part of the continued popularity of this restaurant would have to be the impressive variety of the bill of fare and its proper execution. The Rod 'n Reel certainly lives up to its motto!

Rod 'n Reel
North end of Rogue River Bridge
P.O. Box 58
Wedderburn, OR 97491

247-6823

Hours: Lunch 11 am-2:30 pm weekdays
Dinner 5 pm-10:30 pm every day
Closed Thanksgiving, Christmas Eve and Day

Libations: Full wine list, cocktails, and beer

Payment: VISA, Mastercharge, American Express, Diners, and Carte Blanche

Reservations: Suggested

Rod 'n Reel Stuffed Squid

Sauce

1½-2 pounds cleaned squid hoods
4 tablespoons olive oil
1 small onion, chopped
2 cloves garlic, chopped
a few sprigs fresh parsley, chopped
1 No. 2½ can crushed tomatoes (approximately 3-3½ cups)
salt and pepper to taste

Sauté in oil the onion, garlic and parsley. Add tomatoes, salt and pepper. Cook on low heat approximately 1 hour. If too thick, ½ cup water can be added.

Squid

1 cup coarse bread crumbs
1 teaspoon chopped fresh parsley
1 egg
1 tablespoon Parmesań cheese
dash garlic powder
salt and pepper to taste

Mix all of the above together and stuff into squid hoods using pastry bag or ice teaspoon. (The longer the stuffing "rests" the better—can be made a day in advance.) Sew hoods across opening. Place into sauce and simmer ½ hour. Serve over spaghetti or rice. Serves 4-6.

Appetizers

Shrimp Cocktail . . . .

Stuffed Clams in the Shell, Six . .
Four . . . .

Crab Cocktail . . . .

Oregon Oysters, ½ Shell, Eight .
Four . . . .

Chef Specialties

FRESH BAKED STUFFED ENGLISH SOLE, Stuffed with Shrimp, Cooked in White Wine . . . .

BAKED SCAMPI, Very Large, Tender Shell Fish, Relative to the Shrimp . .

FRESH OREGON OYSTERS, Sauteed in White Wine . . . .

RED SNAPPER, Nantua, Baked Snapper Covered with Shrimp Meat and a Creamy Sauce, Served Only When Fresh . . . .

BAKED STUFFED TROUT, Stuffed with Shrimp and Crab . . . .

CHATEAUBRIAND

A Dinner for 2 - Filet Cooked as You Like It, Planked with Asparagus Spears, Baked Stuffed Potato, Broiled Tomato and Fresh Button Mushrooms - Advance Notice Please

Menu for Petite Ladies

LOBSTER TAIL, Baked in Butter, Drawn Butter, Lemon Wedge . . . .

DELMONICO STEAK, 8 oz., Choice Beef . . . .

Your Choice of the Above Entrees Will Include Something to Nibble on, Homemade Soup, Salad, Your Choice of Dressing, Potato and Coffee

Choice Beef Dinners

DELMONICO, Eye of the Rib . . . .

NEW YORK STEAK . . . .

FILET MIGNON, Tenderloin Butterfly Wrapped in Bacon . . . .

CHOICE GROUND BEEF, One Half Pound, Fresh Mushrooms in Burgundy Sauce . . . .

BEEF BURGUNDY, Choice Cuts in Filet Mignon, Fresh Mushrooms and Scallions, Sauteed in Burgundy Sauce . . . .

BEEF AND REEF, Filet Mignon and Lobster Tail . . . .

Seafood Dinners

RAZOR CLAMS, Grilled and Tender . . . .

SALMON STEAK, The Chinook, Fresh and Juicy, a Real Treat . . . .

ABALONE, Treasure of the Deep . . . .

FILET OF SOLE, Delicious, Fresh White Fish, Lightly Breaded and Grilled .

BAKED HALIBUT MEUNIÈRE . . . .

JUMBO PRAWNS, Breaded Lightly and Deep Fried . . . .

EASTERN SCALLOPS, Tender, Sweet, Breaded and Deep Fried or Baked in Wine . . . .

GRILLED OYSTERS, Fresh Pacific Oysters, Lightly Breaded . . . .

TWO BAKED LOBSTER TAILS . . . .

REEF AND BEEF, Baked Lobster Tail and Grilled Choice Filet Mignon . .

ADMIRAL'S DELIGHT, Fresh Grilled Oysters and Baked Lobster Tail .

MIXED FRY, Prawn, Scallops, Salmon, Oyster and White Fish, Breaded and Deep Fried . . . .

Your Choice of the Above Entrees Will Include Something to Nibble on, Homemade Soup, Salad, Your Choice of Dressing, Potato and Coffee

VISA . . . MASTER CHARGE . . . AX . . . DC . . . CB . . .

Jot's RESORT

PLACIDLY situated on the lower end of the Rogue River is Jot's Resort. The Giottonini family has grown up with the river, and they are as much a part of it as it is of them. Jot's Restaurant is a favorite haunt of locals as well as visitors. Fronting on the bay, patrons watch pelicans and sea lions play in the harbor while they dine. It's as if Jot's reputation is at stake with each dinner served; care is taken in both preparation and service. Jot's is a must on the sportman's and nature lover's—as well as the epicure's—list of places to go.

Jot's Resort
North End Rogue River Bridge on Highway 101
Wedderburn, OR 97491

247-6676 X 283

Hours: 7 am-10 pm daily
No holiday closures

Libations: Full wine list, cocktails, and beer

Payment: VISA, Mastercharge, Diners, American Express, and personal checks with ID

Reservations: Suggested

Jot's
Scallops di Stecchi

32 large scallops
24 medium sized mushroom caps
½ cup butter, melted
garlic powder
paprika
1 cup white wine
8 wooden skewers

Alternate 4 scallops and 3 mushrooms on each skewer. Brush with butter and sprinkle with garlic and paprika.

Lay in buttered baking pan and pour wine over and under skewers.

Bake in 450 °F. oven until done, approximately 10 minutes. Serves 4.

Jot's

DINNER MENU

All specialty, seafood and steak entrees include our chilled relish tray, choice of gourmet salad or soup, baked potato, dinner rolls and coffee.

HORS D'OEUVRES

CHILLED VEGETABLE and RELISH TRAY ....

OREGON PACIFIC SHRIMP COCKTAIL SUPREME ....

YAQUINA BAY OYSTERS LIMONE ....

YAQUINA BAY OYSTER COCKTAIL SUPREME ....

CHILLED JUMBO PRAWNS AL BOLLIRE ....

DUNGENESS CRAB COCKTAIL SUPREME 5 oz. ....

SAVORIES

CAULIFLOWER AL FORMAGGIO ....

CORN ON THE COB ....

BROILED TOMATO GRATINO ....

ASPARAGUS SPEARS PARMESAN ....

SAUTE MUSHROOMS AL VIN ....

SOUPS AND SALADS

Includes dinner roll or crackers and butter

CLAM CHOWDER ....

SOUP DU JOUR ....

Our special recipe soup of the day.

TOSSED VEGETABLE SALAD ....

OREGON PACIFIC SHRIMP LOUIS ....

DUNGENESS CRAB LOUIS ....

SEAFOODS

RED SNAPPER 6 oz. ....

Flavorful fillets of grilled red snapper from the blue Pacific. "Canary" and "Rasphead" rockfish, alias "Red Snapper", in the waters surrounding our Rogue River reef, afford the sportsman some of the best bottom fishing anywhere. No licenses are required to fish these colorful lunkers weighing up to 23 pounds!

TROUT ALMONDINE 2 pcs. - 9 oz. ....

Delicious grilled trout from local streams. Oregon trout fishing is unexcelled and the Rogue River is world famous for its fall and winter runs of steelhead (sea-run rainbow trout). Flyfishing for "steelies" in the Rogue reaches a peak in September and October, but the big winter steelhead are taken December through February, and range from 10 to 25 pounds or more!

OYSTERS 5 pcs. - 10 oz. ....

Succulent grilled oysters from the brackish estuaries along Oregon's scenic coast. Oysters are "farmed" in the stoney bays where the proper mingling of salt and fresh waters creates a perfect environment. As you travel north, take time to visit the oyster farms in Coos and Yaquina Bays.

RAZOR CLAMS 4 pcs. - 5 oz. ....

Tender grilled razor clams from Oregon's sandy beaches. Locally, clam diggers can find these delicious soft shelled clams at Myers Creek and Bailey beaches on any low minus tide. The best clamming is in the spring of the year just before the razors spawn. The legal limit is the first 24 dug, regardless of size.

SCALLOPS 7 pcs. - 6 oz. ....

Sweet juicy deep-fried scallops from the rocky reefs off Oregon's shoreline. Scallops abound in the deep coves along the coast, and the sportsman may dive for a daily bag limit of 24 "rock scallops" with no size limit. Remember that no shellfish may be harvested from within the boundaries of any state park.

SEA & SURF PLATE 4 oz. Snapper/2 oz. Scallops/2 Oysters ....

A tantalizing combination of local seafoods including red snapper, oysters, scallops, and shrimp from Oregon's beaches and reefs.

SALMON (in season) 8 oz. ....

Delicious grilled salmon steaks from our local commercial fisheries. Chinook, the largest of the six species of Pacific salmon, are abundant in the waters of the famous Rogue River with spring, summer and fall runs. The sportsman will never forget a battle with one of these silver beauties. You can join our Rogue River Salmon Club by catching a "button fish" weighing 30 to 50 plus pounds; we added over 80 members last year!

PRAWNS 5 pcs. - 5 oz. ....

Tender juicy deep-fried prawns, imported from Mexico. This large Mexican shrimp species is not found in our area, but our local cocktail-sized shrimp abound along the Oregon coast. Be sure to stop at a nearby commercial cannery and watch the shrimp boats unload.

LOBSTER 9 oz. ....

Delightful broiled South Pacific lobster tail, an imported delicacy.

STEAKS

PETITE TOP SIRLOIN STEAK 6 oz. ....

A petite portion of boneless, juicy beef, char-grilled to your taste.

TERIYAKI STEAK 8 oz. ....

Choice boneless beef from Eastern Oregon's vast ranch lands. This flavorful cut is char-grilled to your liking.

NEW YORK CUT STEAK 10 oz. ....

The finest cut of choice beef, our New York steak is superbly grilled and guaranteed delicious.

ENTREE SPECIALTIES

FRIED CHICKEN ....

Traditional deep-fried Oregon chicken, juicy and tender!

SCALLOPS DI STECCHI 7 oz. ....

Deep sea scallops and button mushrooms marinated in our special wine sauce and spices, then skewered and broiled to perfection.

STEAK & TROUT 4 oz. Trout/6 oz. Top ....

Petite steak and grilled trout almondine - delicious!

STEAK & PRAWNS 4 oz. Prawns/6 oz. Top ....

Deep-fried Mexican prawns and boneless steak, an unbeatable combination!

STEAK & LOBSTER 6 oz. Top/6½ oz. Lobster ....

Oregon prime beef and South Pacific lobster, broiled to perfection.

SWEETS AND ICE DESSERTS

ICE CREAM or SHERBET ....

CHEESE CAKE ....

CREME DE MENTHE PARFAIT ....

PEACH HALVES AMARETTO ....

PEARS AL GRAND MARNIER ....

Captain's Table

VACATION trips to the Oregon coast convinced the Mullins' family that here was the place to combine semi-retirement and new roots. Finding the rambling old house in Gold Beach cinched the decision, and today The Captain's Table stands as a favorite spot for both locals and travelers alike. It's a warm and casual place, marked by collectibles and a relaxing atmosphere. The dining room and lounge both support an extended view of surf and woods. The fare is unpretentious but well prepared, with the emphasis on local seafoods. The Captain's Table is indeed a worthy addition to the better restaurants on the Coast.

The Captain's Table
1295 Highway 101 South
Gold Beach, OR 97444

247-6308

Hours: Summer 5-10 pm Sun.-Thurs.
5-10:30 pm Fri.-Sat.
Winter 5-10 pm Mon.-Sat.
5-9 pm Sun.
Closed Thanksgiving, Easter, Christmas

Libations: Wine list, cocktails, and beer

Payment: VISA, Mastercharge, checks with Bank Guarantee Card

Reservations: Not accepted

The Captain's Table Steamed Clams

2½-3 pounds fresh butter clams
1 ounce white wine
1-2 teaspoons ground garlic
1 ounce lemon juice
1 ounce salad oil
drawn butter
lemon slices

Place clams in steamer with approximately ½ gallon water. Be sure water does not boil clams. Add wine, garlic, lemon juice and oil. Steam clams until just open—serve with drawn butter and lemon slices. Serves 2.

Captain's Table

...All dinners include a large salad mixed with
assorted fresh vegetables, bread and butter,
our own special rice pilaf or baked potato.
(Only the finest ingredients available are used)!

Small Sirloin Steak
Top Sirloin Steak
Teriyaki Sirloin Steak
New York Steak
Filet Mignon
Ground Sirloin
Beef-Kabob (bell peppers, onions, mushrooms)
Chicken Teriyaki
Prime Rib (while still available)
The Captain's Cut
The Shanghai Cut

Alaskan King Crab Legs
Scallop-Kabob (bacon, bell pepper, onion)
Shrimp (plain or teriyaki)
Fish of the Day
Salmon (fresh in season)
Stuffed Trout
Pot of Steamed Clams
Australian Lobster Tail
Combinations:
Seafood Combo (broiled scallops, shrimp, king crab legs)
Steak and Crab
Steak and Lobster

A LA CARTE

Sauteed Mushrooms
Artichoke
Vegetables for two
Pot of Steamed Clams
Salad (includes bread and butter)

The Recipes

"He was a bold man that first eat an oyster."

Jonathan Swift

ONE of our favorite things in life is to savor the cuisine of a talented and creative chef while being pampered in a fine restaurant. As you have no doubt gathered by now, the Oregon coast offers a wide array of opportunities for doing just that. However, there are times when nothing can quite equal the pleasures of a home cooked meal, and here again the coast doesn't disappoint. You'll discover a multitude of fine seafood markets carrying both local and imported varieties to accommodate even the most discriminating tastes. So, now that your appetite for seafoods has been whetted, try your hand at preparing some of the many delectable species available—or, better yet, go catch or dig your own!

We feel the introductory details of just how to approach fish and shellfish and the accompanying recipes will more than adequately arm you to visit the seafood market, confident in the knowledge that you can take home such oddities as the geoduck and not be stymied by that age-old question, "Now what do I do?" We would offer only two words of advice about what to do: Be Imaginative! Throw caution to the wind! Don't be caught off guard by such old wives' tales as, "Steamer clams were meant to be steamed and served with bowls of melted butter!" There is a whole world of versatility in fish and shellfish cookery that remains generally untouched through lack of daring and imagination.

This, then, was our guiding philosophy in selecting and developing recipes for our guide book—never to underestimate the endless variety of possibilities for deliciously rendering the many treasures of the fresh and salt waters of the Oregon coast. So, if you are looking for your standard, all-time favorite recipes, this probably is not the place. But, if you are seeking to enlarge and broaden your culinary horizons with a kaleidoscope of surprises, Bon Appetit!

The First Step: Shopping

Select only the freshest fish and shellfish for your purchase. Be alert for fish whose flesh springs back when touched, whose scales cling (in most species), whose eyes are bright and bulging, and whose smell is fragrantly of the sea. Avoid fish that droop over the counter and whose stomach area is tinged with green or black. A fish watery and fibrous in appearance has been held too long and should be quickly passed over. When shopping for shellfish, be just as choosy. Steamer clams, geoducks, and mussels should be alive and responsive to the touch. Crabs, lobsters, and oysters also should be alive until cooked or killed just before cooking. Crayfish need to be dropped live into boiling broth. Avoid commercially frozen seafood of any kind if at all possible.

The Basic Forms of Fish

You will note that fish are available for purchase in different forms. Listed below are the more common forms and some of their basic characteristics.

The Whole Fish. Usually uncleaned, just as it came from the water. Needs to be scaled and eviscerated before preparing. Sometimes subject to tainting of flavor due to the lack of cleaning. Only about 45 percent edible. 1½ pounds of whole fish yield 2 servings.

The Drawn Fish. Has entrails removed. Needs only to be scaled before preparing. 50 percent edible.

The Dressed Fish. Drawn fish with scales, head, tail, and fins removed. Ready to cook as is. 70 percent edible.

Steaks. Cross-section cuts of a dressed fish, about ¾-1 inch thick, commonly with skin and bones still intact. Ready for preparing as is, 85 percent edible. 1 pound of steaks serves 2.

Fillets. Sides of fish, typically boneless and skinless, and ready to cook. 100 percent edible. ¾ pound of fillets yields 2 servings.

Preliminary Preparation of Fish

To Dress a Fish: Remove scales by using a straight, sharp knife. Begin at tail, working towards head, slanting the knife slightly towards yourself to prevent scales from flying. Begin removal of dorsal and anal fins by making a parallel cut along both sides about ½ inch deep. Lay fish on back and make a deep cut behind vent. Slide knife forward to pectoral fin (the fins on the bottom side of the fish, just behind the head). Place fish on side and make deep cut behind pectoral fin. Repeat on other side. Take hold of head, and pulling upwards, break backbone and remove head. Pull off pectoral and pelvic fins and remove entrails. In salmon and many other species, a membrane containing blood will remain along the backbone; open this with a knife slit and scrape it out with a knife or spoon. Remove dorsal and anal fins with pliers. Cut off tail.

To Fillet a Dressed Fish: Set fish on its side. Using a very sharp knife inserted at tail, make a definite cut through flesh along backbone to just behind head area. Slide knife along backbone to other side and cut flesh away, lifting flesh with free hand so that you are eventually able to lift the entire side of the fish away from the bone structure in one piece. Turn and repeat procedure on other side of fish.

To Skin a Dressed Fish: Some prefer to retain skin on the fish, as this may hold in moisture during the cooking. Others say the skin makes the flesh taste "too fishy." If you wish to discard the skin, simply lay fish, skin side down. Holding onto the tail, insert knife flat against skin and push towards head section, freeing skin and flesh. Try using a little salt on the tip of the knife if it seems to drag.

To Bone or Butterfly a Fish: Set fish back down. Remove gills. Turn fish over so back is up. With a very sharp knife, insert at head and cut between backbone and flesh on one side. Repeat on other side taking care not to cut through flesh to outside. Snip backbone at tail and head with scissors or knife and discard along with viscera. Cut off fins. Rinse.

Any lingering fish odors can be removed from your hands by washing with vinegar or rubbing with salt and then washing with water. Deodorize pans by boiling with vinegar or salt water.

The Basic Types of Fish Cookery

When it comes to cooking, fish can be divided into two categories: the lean and the fat, the essential difference between them being the addition of moisture when preparing lean fish. Whereas fat fish do not require moisture to be added during cooking, lean fish demand some kind of moisture to retain their desirable qualities. The fat fish or oily meated fish category is dominated by salmon, steelhead, trout, and tuna. The lean fish or dry meated fish category encompasses such varieties as cod, flounder, halibut (steaks), red snapper, rockfish, sea bass, smelt, sturgeon, and shellfish. You will notice that the following recipe section has been separated into these two groups on the basis of fat and lean fish. This was done primarily to encourage an interchange of fish in the recipes. For example, the cashew coating would be equally interesting using sole or rockfish. Many of the shellfish recipes can also be adjusted to accommodate another kind of meat, as employing scallops in the Stir Fried Geoduck with Ham and Almonds. For best results in substituting fish in a recipe, be sure you select a type of fish from the same category.

Cooking fish is no mystery when you realize the two different types of fish and the basic cooking methods briefly detailed below. Do remember, however, that no matter what method you select, the prime goal is to cook only until the fish becomes opaque or flakes. Test for doneness by inserting a fork tine in the thickest portion of the fish and lifting up. The flesh is fully cooked when it comes up in layers. Keep in mind that the cook's task is twofold when preparing fish and shellfish. It is not only to protect the fragile texture of the product but also to enhance and complement its basic flavor, not to disguise it.

Baking. Fat fish are best for baking because there is not the concern for loss of moisture. In an oven preheated to 350°F., place fish that has been brushed with oil or sauced. Do not turn fish. Plan on 15 minutes for fillets or steaks, 50 minutes for a 4-pound dressed fish. Add on 25 minutes for stuffed fish. See Tuna Roast.

Broiling, Grilling and Barbecuing. Fish are cooked very quickly, so be attentive. Brush fish with oil or sauce and set on hot, well-oiled grill. Check every 10 minutes or so for doneness. If oven broiling, lay on oiled aluminum foil, brush with oil, and place about 2-3 inches from heat source. See Barbecue Butterflied Trout.

Deep Frying. Drop battered pieces of fish into oil preheated to 375°F. Fry until golden, 3-5 minutes. The fish is done when it rises to the surface. Drain on paper towels. Oil can be strained and reused because it picks up little, if any, fish odor. Freshen, if desired, by cooking potatoes or a few slices of ginger root in it. Use only the best quality oil for the best results. See Robin's Deep Fried Steelhead.

Oven Frying. Set large shallow pan in 500°F. oven with 2-3 tablespoons oil or clarified butter until hot and melted. Remove and place dipped and coated fish into pan. Turn to coat with oil. Return pan to oven and cook until golden and crisp. Do not turn fish. Allow 5 minutes for thinner pieces and up to 15 minutes for thicker pieces. Fish can also be coated, then drizzled with oil or melted butter, set on pan and cooked at 500°F. for similar results. Either method simulates pan frying. See Nut Coated Rockfish.

Pan Frying. Dip fish into liquid and then into breading, or dry (so as to prevent splattering and partial steaming) and fry in sizzling oil or clarified butter. Turn once and cook until golden and crisp. Less than sizzling oil will produce a soggy, greasy product. Choose an oil that is not too strongly flavored—one whose flavor will not interfere with the subtle flavor of the fish. See Gingered Trout.

Stir Frying. This is the Oriental technique of preparing foods over a high heat, stirring constantly, with a minimum amount of oil. Cooking time is short to preserve the product's initial color, flavor, texture, and nutrient value. See Stir Fried Squid with Vegetables.

Poaching. This is the method most acclaimed by purists and gourmets to bring out the prime flavor of even the most delicate of fish. The fish is lowered into simmering broth that includes water, acid ingredient, vegetables, and spices, and cooked until flaky. See Poached Fish.

Smoking. A method of preserving fish such as salmon, smelt, sturgeon, steelhead and trout. The fish is first soaked in a salt solution, allowed to dry, then placed in container where the smoke both imparts flavor and cooks the fish. See Ernie's Special Smoked Trout.

Steaming. Bring small amount of water to boil in bottom of steamer. Lower heat and set fish fillets or steaks or whole fish with seasonings on greased rack. Cover and steam until flaky, 5-15 minutes. See Steamed Steelhead with Black Beans.

Be on guard to protect your gastronomical creation from being just another colorless piece of fish, as may easily happen without due attention to visual appearance. Pep up the look of your carefully prepared plate by employing herbs, spices, and seeds—but naturally with your own touch of genius.

Traditional seasonings would include basil, bay leaf, chervil, dill weed, marjoram, mint, oregano, paprika, parsley, rosemary, saffron, sage, savory, tarragon, and thyme. Commonly used seeds are dill, fennel, mustard, and sesame. These seeds can be conveniently crushed by placing in blender for a short time.

Wines as well as herbs, spices, and seeds work to bring out the best in fish and shellfish cuisine. In the following recipes you will frequently come across the phrase "white dinner wine" to suggest sauternes (Semillon, Sauvignon Blanc), rhine wines (Riesling, Traminer, Sylvaner) and chablis (Pinot Blanc, Pinot Chardonnay, White Port). Vary your selection in wine to find what pleases you the most.

Refrigeration and Freezing

Ideally, fish and shellfish should be consumed the day they are obtained. If this is not possible, refrigerate for the briefest time possible in a moisture-proof container to prevent transfer of odor and loss of moisture. If the product cannot be consumed in a couple of days, freeze at 0° to -10°F. in meal size portions, labeled as to contents and dated. Fish deteriorates in quality much more rapidly than other meats and needs to be disposed of as soon as possible.

Freezing may be done in several ways. The fish can be frozen unwrapped, then removed from the freezer, dipped in or sprayed with very cold water, forming a thin layer of ice. This process is repeated until ⅛ inch glaze is built up. Wrap and freeze fish.

OR

Lean fish may be dipped in a mixture of ½ cup salt and 1 quart water for 20 seconds then wrapped and frozen.

OR

Fat fish may be dipped in a mixture of 1½ teaspoons ascorbic acid in 1 quart water, wrapped and frozen.

OR

Fish may be dropped into rinsed milk containers, filled with water (some people add a drop of lemon juice) to completely cover the fish; then close the containers, and freeze. This last method has been most successful for us. Whereas the former methods only tend to preserve the fish for several months, the block of ice method seems to hold them almost indefinitely with small loss in original flavor and texture.

Thaw frozen fish slowly, in the refrigerator if possible, to prevent excess leakage. If time is critical, thaw under cold, running water. When fish is in block of ice, tear carton away from ice, set block in colander, and set in bowl to catch thawing water. It is extremely important not to allow fish to sit in water. Figure on 4 hours to thaw 1 pound of fish at room temperature and 8-24 hours in refrigerator.

Shellfish may be frozen in similar fashion. Steamer clams, mussels, oysters, scallops, and shrimp can be removed from the shell, placed in freezer containers, covered with court bouillon, their own juices, or water and frozen. Unshelled clams, mussels, and shrimp can be frozen by slipping into plastic bags. Crabs and lobsters are most successfully frozen by cooking, shelling, and covering with liquid and freezing in a block. Crayfish should be cooked and frozen whole in water or broth. Ground clams can be packed into freezer containers and sealed. Octopus should be cooked and cleaned and frozen in block of ice. Squid should be cleaned, covered with liquid, and frozen in block of ice.

Fat or Oily Meated Fish

THE GOURMET ROOM'S SALMON QUENELLES

4 ounces salmon meat, clean and deboned, ground up
2 ounces coffee cream (half & half)
2 ounces egg whites
1 ounce butter, melted
1 or 2 shallots, peeled and chopped, sautéed
salt
pepper, white
lemon juice to taste
MSG

Combine all ingredients and puree in blender. Shape with spoon and poach in salted boiling water. Cool in water.

Prepare salmon aspic by combining salmon bones, cold water, bay leaf, peppercorns, celery, onions, and carrot (bouquet garni) and bring to a boil. Simmer for not more than 15 minutes. Strain. Test a small amount in freezer. If it does not jell (insufficient bones), fortify with unflavored gelatin. Season to taste (MSG, salt, Tabasco).

Pour small amount in container (cup or champagne glass). Let set. Put cold drained quenelles on top, garnish. Carefully pour balance of liquid aspic on top. Chill—do not freeze. Preferred garnish: fresh dill weed, caviar, truffle.

LA PLAZA RESTAURANT BAKED SALMON

1 salmon, steelhead or large trout
mayonnaise
lemon
Super Salad Seasoning or Salad Elegance

Fillet fish and place skin side down on flat pan which has been lined with aluminum foil. Squeeze lemon on fish and wait 5 minutes for lemon to soak into fish.

With a spatula, spread a thin layer of mayonnaise over fish, and then sprinkle generously with salad seasoning. This will add flavor and also produce a nice color when fish is baked. Place fish in 375 °F. oven.

A 5-pound fish will take approximately 30 minutes.

THE CAPTAIN'S TABLE SALMON BELLEVIEW

Fillet of Chinook salmon
2 tablespoons honey

Broil fillet at low heat until white oil begins to show. Top with 1-2 tablespoons of honey-almond sauce. Place salmon with sauce in oven for approximately 5 minutes at 325 °F. Serves 4.

HONEY-ALMOND SAUCE: Saute almonds in clear butter until golden in color. Add 2 tablespoons honey. Heat until simmering.

FESTIVE SALMON SANDWICHES

1 pound salmon, cooked and flaked
½ cup sour cream
½ teaspoon dill weed
1 tablespoon chopped parsley
½ teaspoon ground pepper
1 small onion, diced fine
2 egg whites, beaten stiff
cocktail rye bread

Combine salmon, sour cream, dill

weed, parsley, pepper and onion. Fold in beaten egg whites. Spread on rye slices and toast under broiler until puffy and lightly toasted.

Makes a wonderful party hors d'oeuvre or tasty accompaniment to plain soup. Serves 2-8.

SALMON PICNIC SALAD

½ pound cooked salmon, broken into chunks
2 hard-boiled eggs, chopped
2 tablespoons sliced pimento
8 ounces water chestnuts, thinly sliced
¼ cup sliced green onions
½ cup sliced celery
⅓ cup mayonnaise
1 tablespoon prepared mustard

Combine and toss salmon, eggs, pimento, water chestnuts, green onions, and celery. Stir together mayonnaise and mustard. Fold into salmon mixture and refrigerate overnight to blend flavors. Serves 4.

COVERED BARBECUE WHOLE SALMON

1 whole salmon, cleaned and scaled, rinsed and patted dry, dorsal and pectoral fins removed.
Protect head and tail by wrapping in oiled paper then in foil.
cherry or apple wood chunks, slightly dampened to produce more smoke
salt and pepper
onion and lemon slices
parsley sprigs

Sprinkle cavity of salmon with salt and pepper and line with lemon and onion slices and parsley sprigs. Lightly brush grill and fish with oil.

Wrap fish body with expanded aluminum strip obtained from hardware store. Lay fish on grill and throw handfuls of wood chips onto coals.

Barbecue very slowly until fish reaches 120°F. at thickest part.

OR

Remove head from fish. Place fish on oiled aluminum foil. Fill cavity with onion and lemon slices and parsley sprigs. Sprinkle with salt and pepper. Enclose fish in foil.

Place over coals, turn every 10 minutes until done, about ½ hour.

Serve by opening foil, lifting off skin, and then spooning portions of flesh away from the bone.

STEAMED STEELHEAD WITH BLACK BEANS

4 steelhead steaks or fillets
2 tablespoons fermented black beans, washed
1 clove garlic
4 tablespoons soy sauce
2 thin slices fresh ginger root, chopped fine
1 tablespoon oil
1 teaspoon brown sugar
2 tablespoons snipped chives

Pound together the beans, garlic, soy sauce, ginger, oil, and sugar. Rub mixture evenly over fish.

Place fish on holder over boiling water and steam 8-12 minutes or until fish flakes. Remove from steamer and sprinkle with snipped chives. Serves 4.

STEELHEAD IN ALMOND-BRANDY SAUCE

4 large steelhead fillets or steaks cut into ½-inch-wide strips
1 cup slivered almonds
¾ pound sliced mushrooms
⅓ cup brandy

2 tablespoons lemon juice
1 cup whipping cream
4 tablespoons butter

Melt butter and brown almonds. Remove almonds and set aside. Add mushrooms to butter and cook until all juices are gone. Remove mushrooms and set aside.

Sauté steelhead strips in same butter, adding more if necessary. Pour in brandy when all pieces are cooked, and flame. Sprinkle with lemon juice. Remove and keep warm on serving platter.

Return mushrooms to pan along with whipping cream. Boil rapidly until cream is full rich golden color.

Stir in almonds and pour mixture over steelhead strips and serve 4.

PICKLED STEELHEAD

2½ pound chunk of steelhead, with skin and bones still intact
16 whole allspice
4 whole peppercorns
1 teaspoon salt
1 small onion, sliced
1 whole lemon, sliced
1 bay leaf
1½ cups white vinegar
8 tablespoons sugar
thin onion slices

Place steelhead in saucepan to fit and cover with water. Add 8 of the allspice, all the peppercorns, salt, lemon slices, and the small sliced onion.

Bring to boil and simmer 5 minutes. Discard liquid and spices and allow steelhead to cool. Skin and bone fish, breaking into chunks.

Arrange 3 pint jars with alternating layers of steelhead and onion rings. Combine and bring to boil the vinegar, sugar, remaining allspice, and bay leaf. Pour over fish.

Seal jars in hot water bath or keep well-covered in refrigerator for several days. Makes 3 pints.

ROBIN'S DEEP FRIED STEELHEAD

2 pounds steelhead, skinned and boned, cut into 1-inch squares
1 cup flour
2 teaspoons baking powder
1 teaspoon salt
1 teaspoon sugar
1 cup flat beer
1½ teaspoons oil

Stir together the flour, baking powder, salt, and sugar. Blend beer and oil and mix into dry ingredients.

Dip steelhead squares into batter and fry in oil preheated to 375°F. until golden. Serves 4.

BARBECUE SMOKED STEELHEAD FILLETS

4 steelhead fillets with the skin still intact
½ cup butter, melted with a little lemon juice added
apple or cherry wood chips or chunks

Oil 4 pieces of aluminum foil, each large enough to hold one fillet. Set each fillet on foil, skin side down, then place on barbecue grill over moderately warm coals. Brush with lemon juice and butter mixture.

Quickly throw handful of wood chips or chunks onto coals, and cover barbecue (if your barbecue doesn't come with cover, try using a large piece of aluminum foil to act as a lid). Occasionally baste fish and add more chips.

Should take 20-30 minutes to bring fish to flake stage. Serves 4.

STEELHEAD TACOS

1 pound cooked steelhead, skinned and boned, broken into chunks

½ cup sour cream or unflavored yogurt
½ cup sliced green onions
½ cup thinly sliced cucumbers
½ cup thinly sliced radishes
½ cup thinly sliced lettuce
8 flour tortillas
bottled taco sauce
salad oil

Fry tortillas in salad oil until lightly brown. Fill with steelhead chunks and sprinkle with condiments. Accompany with taco sauce. Serves 4.

HAYSTACK HOUSE STUFFED TROUT EN PAPILLOTE

6 boned trout (8 ounces or up)
12 ounces cocktail shrimp
12 ounces crab meat
½ pound butter
1½ cups celery (diced)
1 cup onion (diced)
1 cup chablis
½ teaspoon poultry seasoning
½ teaspoon white pepper
6 paper hearts cut from parchment or butchers' paper approx. 18 inches x 16 inches

In a heavy skillet melt butter; add celery and onion. Sauté until almost transparent. Add poultry seasoning and white pepper; stir in well. Add shrimp and crab. Add wine to the mixture and allow to simmer, stirring occasionally, until liquid is reduced by half. Remove from heat. Allow to cool.

Stuff trout liberally with mixture. Brush butter on smooth or shiny side of paper. Place trout on heart with back next to creased side and tail facing pointed end of heart. Squeeze a wedge of fresh lemon over trout. Seal trout in paper by starting at top or head and folding over 1 inch of the edges all the way around and crimping them together. Place on baking sheet in preheated oven (350 °F.) for 20 minutes.

To serve, lay the papillotes on individual serving plates and, with the point of a paring knife, cut the upper paper about three-fourths of the way around, making the cut just inside the crimped edge of the lower part of the heart. The fish is eaten directly from the paper.

STUFFED TROUT

4-6 trout, cleaned
½ pound bacon, fried crisp and crumbled
3 tablespoons bacon drippings
1 onion, chopped
1 tablespoon chopped parsley
1 egg blended with 1 tablespoon milk
1 cup bread crumbs
6 tablespoons butter

Sauté onion in bacon drippings until golden. Remove from heat and stir in crumbled bacon and parsley.

Divide among trout and fill cavities with mixture. Secure with toothpick or tie closed.

Roll in egg mixture and then in bread crumbs. Melt butter in skillet and sauté trout until fish flakes. Serves 4-6.

GINGERED TROUT

4-6 trout, cleaned
½ cup salad oil
1 cup flour
3 tablespoons minced ginger root
¼ cup brown sugar
¼ cup white vinegar
¾ cup water
⅓ cup sliced green onion
2 teaspoons cornstarch
⅓ cup water

Brush trout with oil and roll in flour. Fry in hot oil until golden.

Meanwhile prepare sauce by simmering together ginger root, sugar, vinegar, ¾ cup water, and green onions for 15 minutes. Stir cornstarch into remaining water and then into ginger sauce. Bring mixture to boil and cook until thickened.

Serve in individual bowls as dipping sauce for trout. Serves 4-6.

ERNIE'S SPECIAL SMOKED TROUT

trout, cleaned
rock salt
brown sugar
apple or hickory wood chips

Add enough rock salt to cold water so that only a dime-sized portion of an egg floating in it will be above water level.

Blend in 1 pound of brown sugar for each 6 gallons of water.

Soak fresh fish in this solution for up to 30 hours; frozen fish for up to 15 hours.

Remove from salt-sugar solution and air dry until glaze forms on fish, usually ½ to 1 hour.

Smoke 5-10 hours using apple or hickory wood chips or any nonresinous wood, being sure to discard bark which might impart a bitter flavor. Trout are done smoking when dorsal fin easily pulls away from the fish.

This same recipe can be used for salmon and steelhead, in which case the end of smoking would be determined by your personal taste.

BARBECUED BUTTERFLIED TROUT

4 trout, cleaned
2 cups homemade or prepared Italian style oil and vinegar salad dressing

Bone and butterfly trout. Marinate in salad dressing for 1-2 hours. Drain.

Place each trout, skin side down on barbecue, and cook over charcoal until flesh firms, about 5-15 minutes.

Brush once or twice with salad dressing. Serves 2-4.

SOY TROUT

4 trout, cleaned
2 teaspoons minced ginger root
4 tablespoons brown sugar
¼ cup white dinner wine
¼ teaspoon powdered garlic
½ cup salad oil
1 teaspoon paprika
¾ cup cornmeal
¼ cup flour
¼ cup finely chopped nuts, such as walnuts or almonds

Blend ginger root, sugar, wine, garlic, and oil. Pour over trout and marinate 1-2 hours.

Combine paprika, cornmeal, flour, and nuts; roll fish in mixture to coat.

Grill or pan fry fish. Serves 2-4.

TUNA ROAST

thick tuna steak, small whole tuna or chunk of tuna
cloth wrung out in vinegar
melted butter
seasoning salt and pepper
paprika

Wipe tuna with cloth. Set on rack in oven pan. Roast at 350°F. for 20 minutes.

Pull off and discard fat and skin. Brush with butter and season with salt and pepper. Sprinkle with paprika.

Continue baking until fish flakes, figuring 15 minutes per pound of tuna.

TUNA CHOWDER WITH LEMON BREAD

2 7-ounce cans of tuna, well drained, OR
1 pound cooked tuna meat, broken into chunks
¼ cup butter
1 large onion, chopped
1½ tablespoons flour
2 cups light chicken broth
2 cups diced potatoes
1¼ cups diced carrots
¾ cup sliced celery
1 cup green peas
2 cups half & half or milk
¼ teaspoon each basil and thyme leaves

Melt the butter in saucepan. Add onions and sauté until golden. Stir in flour and cook until bubbly. Gradually add chicken broth, stirring constantly until thick. Add vegetables and simmer 20 minutes. Add tuna, half & half, basil and thyme leaves and cook until warmed through over low heat. Serves 4-6 accompanied by lemon muffins.

Lemon Muffins: Blend: ¼ cup butter, 1 teaspoon lemon juice, 1 teaspoon fresh lemon rind, ½ teaspoon snipped parsley. Spread on halves of 3 sourdough muffins and broil until well toasted.

BABY TUNA BAKE

2-3 pound baby tuna, cleaned, with head and tail left on fish
2 tablespoons butter
1 large green onion, sliced
½ cup dry vermouth

Oil baking pan and add fish, upside down, so that body cavity is opened slightly. Sprinkle cavity with onions and dot with butter. Pour vermouth over all. Bake at 425°F. for 20-30 minutes. Serves 3-4. Marinated Carrot Salad compliments this clean treatment of tuna.

Marinated Carrot Salad: Simmer ¾ pound carrots (cut into ¼" slices) in boiling water for 10 minutes. Drain and cool. Combine with 2 slices ginger root, 6-ounce jar marinated artichoke hearts, 4 ounces of sliced water chestnuts, ¼ pound quartered mushrooms, ½ green pepper (coarsely chopped), 20 pitted ripe olives (cut in half), juice of 2 limes, ⅛ teaspoon powdered garlic, ¼ teaspoon dried sage leaves and ⅛ teaspoon thyme leaves. Refrigerate, well covered, overnight.

Lean or Dry Meated Fish

POACHED FISH

Whole fish or fillets of lean or fat fish (fat fish must be wrapped in cheesecloth or parchment to prevent fish from flaking apart during cooking process and to prevent breakage when removing from cooking liquid)
1 quart water, or just enough to barely cover fish
1 sliced onion
8 peppercorns
juice of 1 lemon
1 bay leaf
1 teaspoon salt
½ cup white dinner wine

Combine all ingredients except fish to form a court bouillon. Bring to boil, lower heat to simmer, and place either on top of the stove or in oven.

Lower fish into mixture. Liquid should never boil again, or fish will toughen and fall apart. On the other hand, fish must be cooked quickly or it will become rubbery and dry. The temperature is correct when tiny bubbles form and break just below the surface of the liquid.

Cook until fish begins to flake, figuring 10 minutes per pound for whole fish and 5-7 minutes per pound of thin fillets.

Remove fish from liquid and serve hot or cold, alone or with any of the several sauces following.

For variation, try adding parsley, chervil, carrots, dill, thyme, cloves, or celery to the poaching liquid.

SAUCES FOR POACHED FISH

Brandied Butter Sauce: Melt 3 tablespoons butter; add 3 tablespoons lemon juice, 1 cup orange juice, and 2 tablespoons brandy. Bring to boil and cook over high heat 5 minutes. Just before serving, stir in ⅓ cup toasted, slivered almonds. Serve over or alongside fish.

Wine Sauce: Combine 1 tablespoon cornstarch with 1 cup white dinner wine. Melt 2 tablespoons butter and slowly add wine and cornstarch mixture. Cook until clear and thick. Add juice of 1 lemon. Serve alongside fish.

Hollandaise Sauce: Place in top of double boiler 2 egg yolks, ⅛ teaspoon cayenne pepper, 1 tablespoon lemon juice, ¼ teaspoon salt, and ⅓ of a cube of butter. Stir constantly until all butter has melted. Add the second ⅓ of the cube of butter and stir until melted. Add the final ⅓ of the cube and stir until melted. By now the mixture should be thick. Beat until glossy and serve over or alongside the fish.

Brown and Green Fish Sauce: Combine 1½ cups chicken broth, 2 tablespoons soy sauce, and 2 thin slices ginger root and bring to boil. Lower heat and simmer 10 minutes. Remove and discard ginger root. Blend 1 tablespoon cornstarch with 1 tablespoon sherry and add to chicken broth. Cook until thickened. Stir in ¼ pound ham, cut into matchstick size pieces, and ⅓ cup sliced green onions. Cook until heated thoroughly. Serve over or alongside the fish.

Macadamia Nut Butter Sauce: Melt ½ cup butter and stir in ½ cup chopped macadamia nuts. Serve over fish.

FISH STOCK
A Base for Fish Stews and Chowders

2-4 pounds of lean fish bones, heads, and pieces (these can be easily and successfully frozen over a period of time until enough have accumulated to make stock. If fat fish are included, you may find the stock to be quite strong.)
2 quarts of water or water and juices you have retained from cans of fish or from fish that has thawed
½-1 cup white dinner wine
½ lemon, sliced
1 onion, sliced
1 stalk celery, sliced
1 bay leaf
6 white peppercorns
parsley sprigs

Add fish bones and pieces to water. Bring to boil, lower heat, and add remaining ingredients.

Simmer one hour, remembering that cooking too long will produce a bitter stock. Skim several times. Strain, retaining only liquid. Freeze liquid until ready to use.

For variation, other vegetables may be added to stock, but sparingly, as they may darken stock or overpower fish with their own flavor.

Makes about 2 quarts base for fish stews and chowders.

FIDDLERS GREEN CIOPPINO SAUCE

4 stalks of celery (chopped including leaves)
1 medium onion, diced
2 cups white wine (chablis, sauterne)
1 cup water
1 cup oil
3 tablespoons Italian seasoning
1 teaspoon salt
1 teaspoon pepper
1 clove garlic, crushed

Sauté ingredients in double boiler until celery is clear. Add 1 gallon diced tomato in puree. If you can't find that, use 2 cans whole tomatoes and 2 cans of pureé. Mash tomatoes with potato masher.

Cook in double boiler or over slow heat for about 3 hours.

Just before you are ready to serve (25 minutes), add white fish, crab (in shell), clams (little necks in shell), large prawns, oysters. Cooked when fish flakes and clams open. Serve with garlic bread for dunking in sauce.

SEAFOOD RAGOUT

1. **1 teaspoon salt**
1 tablespoon pepper
½ teaspoon grated ginger root (careful, not too much)
1 clove garlic, crushed or chopped
2 teaspoons paprika
1 teaspoon whole thyme
3 tablespoons soy sauce
1 tablespoon cider vinegar
4 cups water
2 cups whole tomatoes, crushed with juice OR 6 medium fresh tomatoes, peeled and seeded

Combine all ingredients, bring to boil, reduce to simmer for additional 15 minutes. Due to spicy nature of the broth it is suggested that vegetables and seafood be lightly poached separately.

2. In equal amounts (1 cup), coarsely chop:

carrots, celery, onions, potatoes

Boil until fork tender; onions should be sautéed till limp!

3. Seafood suggestions:

8 ounces scallops
8 ounces prawns
8 ounces halibut
1 pound steamer clams (hardshells)
8 ounces baby shrimp

Cut halibut to about the same size as the scallops. Combine all ingredients except for baby shrimp. Poach in slightly salted water until steamers open.

Take the cooked vegetables and lay them out in a deep serving dish. Surround and cover with poached fish. Immerse in sauce and top with baby shrimp. Serve with hot garlic French bread.

DORY COVE RON'S SEAFOOD CASSEROLE VICTORIA

10-12 ounce selection of seafood: scallops, shrimp, crab legs, lobster and a white ocean fish. Selection can be varied to accommodate personal taste
1 ounce butter
1 ounce flour
½ onion, finely minced
2 ounces mushrooms, sliced
¼ pint milk or half & half
⅛ pint dry white wine
½ ounce each red and green bell peppers, diced
1 ounce truffles, sliced
salt and white pepper
1 clove garlic, crushed
Fines Herbs
parsley sprigs
lemon wedges

Sauté seafood in one ounce butter;

drain, remove and arrange in a nine inch casserole dish. In remaining liquid, cook onions, mushrooms and peppers until soft. Add the flour. Keeping over moderate heat, add milk and white wine. Stir until smooth and creamy consistency is reached; add seasonings and herbs to taste. Pour over seafood and bake in oven for approximately 12 minutes at 375°F..

Garnish with sliced truffles, parsley and lemon wedges. Serve piping hot.

As an option, finely grated cheese can be added prior to baking. Serves 1.

MANZANITA INN SEAFOOD VERACRUZANO

This recipe is a hybrid of several techniques and ideas worked out at the Inn over a four year period. Portions are not given in the Inn's traditional "eyeball" cooking style. Once the basic sauce, which resembles Ciopinno with a South American touch, is made, the basic meal can be ready in a matter of minutes.

—Sauté (in order, to keep ingredients from turning to mush) fresh onions (chopped), sliced green peppers and sliced mushrooms; use olive oil instead of butter, seasoned with garlic (dried garlic is fine, but if you use a clove, be sure to remove it when the oil is hot).

—When the mushrooms are cooked through and the green pepper and onions are tender, add a small quantity of stewed tomatoes. We sometimes use fresh tomato wedges, but this has to be done carefully to keep the tomatoes from mushing up.

—Simmer lightly until the vegetables are cooked through but distinct. Add pinch of dill, sweet basil, lemon juice and white wine (dry). For a brothier mixture, simply add juice from stewed tomatoes or clam nectar (preferably, a combination of both).

—Put the mixture in a large skillet, and add to it your favorite seafoods . . . bottom fish without bones (chunks of ling cod, slices of sole, snapper fillets); halibut chunks; steamer clams; shrimp; Pacific shrimp; cracked crab; mussels; or any seafood with a good, firm, boneless texture.

—Cover tightly and simmer until done. Generally, the clams will open first, but be sure bottom fish is cooked through.

This dish is exceptionally colorful when served on a bed of white rice or jumbo shell noodles. Done correctly, this is a colorful potpourri of red, white, green and yellow. Garnish with lemon slices.

LEAN FISH WITH CASHEW COAT

2 pounds lean fish fillets (cod, flounder, halibut, etc.), cut into single-serving portions
½ pint sour cream
¾ cup chopped cashews
¼ cup butter

Spread fillets with layer of sour cream on both sides and dip into nuts to cover.

Melt butter, add fillets, and slowly sauté on both sides until cashews are a golden brown color. Serves 4-6.

LEAN FISH WITH POIVRE VERTE

2 pounds lean fish fillets (cod, flounder, halibut, etc.), cut into single-serving portions
½ cup butter
½ cup chopped cashews
3 tablespoons rinsed and drained green peppercorns

Arrange fillets in a well-buttered, shallow baking pan.

Heat butter until just beginning to melt and very soft. Stir in cashews and peppercorns. Spread and pour over fish fillets.

Place 8 inches from heat source in oven and broil until nuts begin to brown.

Change temperature to 500°F. and cook until fish begins to flake.

Baste once or twice with butter mixture and serve to 4 with sauce spooned over fillets.

LEAN FISH WITH FENNEL SEED

1 pound lean fish (cod, flounder, halibut, etc.), cut into serving-size portions
2 tablespoons butter
½ cup slivered almonds
2 green onions, sliced
2 tablespoons sherry, left to sit overnight with 2 slices of fresh ginger
1 tablespoon fennel seed, lightly pounded

Melt butter and add almonds to toast. Remove almonds. Stir in onions, sherry (discarding ginger slices), and fennel seed.

Add fish, turning to coat with sauce. Cover and cook on simmer 5-10 minutes.

Serve on platter with juices spooned over fish and a sprinkling of almonds. Serves 2-3.

LEAN FISH WITH CURRY TOPPING

1 pound lean fish (cod, flounder, halibut, etc.), cut into serving-size portions
1 egg white, beaten stiff
⅔ cup mayonnaise
1 teaspoon curry powder
paprika

Place fish in oven pan that has been lightly buttered. Blend mayonnaise and curry powder and fold into egg white. Spread evenly over fish portions to cover fish completely.

Sprinkle with paprika and bake at 350°F. for 20 minutes or until topping is a buttery-brown color. Serves 2-3.

BAY HOUSE FRESH FISH TEMPURA WITH BASIC SWEET & SOUR SAUCE

Select a pound of fresh fillets (We suggest you use any firm, white bottom fish, such as snapper or cod.) and cut into 1" by 2" strips. Dip into a batter (a commercial Tempura batter mix is fine or consult a recipe from this cookbook). Fry in wok, pan, or deep fryer. Any cooking oil will suffice, but peanut oil is the classic choice. Serves 4.

Basic Sweet & Sour Sauce

¾ cup water
⅓ cup honey
½ cup vinegar
2 tablespoons catsup
2 tablespoons soy sauce
1 tablespoon cornstarch
juice of 3 pressed garlic cloves
sesame seeds
cilantro (Chinese parsley)

Add honey to boiling water and cook a minute to blend. Add vinegar and cook a minute longer. Blend remaining ingredients and about ¼ cup extra water. Stir in as thickening. Pour sauce over fried fish and serve, garnishing with toasted sesame seeds and cilantro.

PERCH IN CREAM SAUCE

2 small whole perch, scaled and cleaned
1 tablespoon lemon juice
flour
¼ cup butter
1 cup white dinner wine
1 cup whipping cream

2 tablespoons sliced green onions

Sprinkle perch with lemon juice and dust with flour. Melt butter in large baking pan in 400°F. oven. Lay fish in melted butter, turn and butter other side. Bake 5-15 minutes or until almost cooked.

Drain off butter and pour wine in pan; heat 10 minutes. Pour in whipping cream and stir in green onions, mixing well. Heat until mixture is warmed through. Serves 2.

NUT COATED ROCKFISH

2 pounds rockfish fillets
½ cup flour
1 teaspoon paprika
1½ cups finely chopped almonds
2 eggs beaten with 2 tablespoons white dinner wine
¼ cup butter, melted

Combine flour, paprika, and chopped almonds. Dip fillets into egg mixture and then into flour mixture.

Place on greased baking sheet, drizzle with butter, and bake at 375°F. about 15 minutes or until flaky. Serves 4-6.

SNAPPER CHARLESTON

½ cup veloute sauce made with Gruyere cheese
6 ounces red snapper
1 slice large peeled tomato
1 tablespoon grated Gruyere cheese
1 teaspoon capers

Place snapper in casserole, pour half the amount of sauce over fish. Sliced tomato goes next, grated cheese on top. Pour remainder of sauce over cheese. Sprinkle with capers on very top.

Bake in 450°F. oven for 10 minutes or until just done. Serves 1.

ROCKFISH TEMPURA

1 pound rockfish fillets, cut into individual serving portions
⅓ cup beer
1 egg, separated
2 teaspoons oil
½ cup flour
½ teaspoon parsley, chopped very fine

Heat oil in deep fat fryer to about 370°F. Combine thoroughly the beer, egg yolk, oil, flour and parsley. Beat egg white until stiff and gently fold into flour mixture. Dip fish pieces into batter and then lower into hot oil. Fry until brown. Drain on absorbent paper. Serves 2, accompanied by Dipping Sauce or bowls of hot Chinese mustard or Red Cocktail Sauce (see Index).

Dipping Sauce: Combine and bring to boil 1 cup clam juice, ¼ cup soy sauce, 2 tablespoons sherry, 1 teaspoon finely chopped ginger root. Simmer a few minutes and allow to cool. Makes 1¼ cups sauce.

SWEET & SOUR ROCKFISH

2 or 3-pound rockfish, cut into individual fillets
3 tablespoons sherry or white dinner wine
¾ cup cornstarch
½ cup sliced green onions
½ cup diced carrots
¼ teaspoon powdered garlic
1½ cups chicken broth
¼ cup oil
½ cup each soy sauce, vinegar, and sugar
3 tablespoons cornstarch in 3 tablespoons water
⅓ cup slivered almonds, toasted

Brush rockfish fillets with sherry and sprinkle with cornstarch. Fry in oil preheated to 375°F. until golden brown. Drain and place on serving platter.

Prepare sauce by heating ¼ cup oil in

saucepan. Stir fry vegetables 1 minute. Add remaining ingredients and cook until sauce boils and thickens. Pour over fish and sprinkle with almonds. Serves 4.

BAKED SEA BASS

1 pound sea bass fillets
4 tablespoons butter
½ teaspoon minced ginger root
2 tablespoons sesame seed, lightly toasted
⅛ teaspoon garlic powder
1 tablespoon snipped chives

Set fillets on oiled baking pan. Soften butter slightly and stir in ginger root, sesame seeds, and garlic powder.

Spread mixture over fillets and bake in 350°F. oven 10-20 minutes, basting occasionally. Serve with pan juices and a sprinkling of chives. Serves 2.

BROILED SEA BASS

1 pound sea bass fillets
½ tablespoon lime juice OR
1 tablespoon lemon juice
1 small onion, thinly sliced
2 tablespoons butter
½ cup white dinner wine
½ tablespoon flour in 2 tablespoons white wine
6 stuffed green olives OR 6 ripe olives, sliced thinly

Arrange fillets in buttered oven dish. Sprinkle with lime or lemon juice; cover with onion slices and dot with butter. Place under broiler and cook, basting with wine, until fish flakes easily. Pour off liquid into saucepan and thicken with flour mixture. Stir in olives and pour sauce over fish. Serves 2-4. Brown rice sprinkled with toasted almonds and parsley is a great side dish for this entree.

Almond Brown Rice: Prepare 1 cup brown rice according to package directions. Sauté ½ cup slivered almonds in 2 tablespoons melted butter. Stir into cooked rice along with 2 tablespoons chopped parsley.

BAKED BASS WITH NUTTY RICE

bass, dressed
butter
Pernod

Certainly a simple recipe but sensational: Place fish in well buttered baking dish and dot with butter. Bake 15 minutes at 400°F., sprinkle generously with Pernod and continue cooking until fish flakes. Serve accompanied with Nutty Rice.

Nutty Rice: Melt 2 tablespoons butter in saucepan. Add 1 cup long grain rice and cook, stirring, until golden in color. Add 2 cups hot chicken broth, cover and simmer 15-20 minutes. Fluff with fork. Stir in 1 cup toasted nuts (cashews, almonds, etc. or a combination of nuts) and serve with any simple fish dish.

CHINESE SMELT

1-2 pounds smelt, cleaned
¼ cup soy sauce
½ cup cornstarch
2 tablespoons oil
1 teaspoon minced ginger root
1 carrot, diced
¼ cup sliced celery
¼ cup sliced green onions
½ cup green peas
1 tablespoon cornstarch in 3 tablespoons vinegar
1 tablespoon soy sauce
1 tablespoon tomato-based seafood sauce
½ cup chicken broth
1 tablespoon sherry
3 tablespoons brown sugar

Brush smelt with soy sauce and roll in cornstarch. Fry in hot oil until crisp and golden. Place on heated platter.

Prepare sauce by heating 2 tablespoons oil in saucepan. Add ginger root, carrot, celery, green onion, and peas, and stir fry until all are heated through. Add remaining ingredients and bring to boil.

Cook until thickened. Pour over smelt and serve 4-6.

GRILLED SMELT

1 pound smelt, cleaned and wiped with damp cloth
2 large tomatoes, sliced
1 onion, sliced
oil

Lay out smelt on a generously oiled sheet of aluminum foil. Spread with a layer of tomato and onion slices. Enclose fish in foil and secure tightly. Grill over medium coals for 12-15 minutes, turning once. Remember fish cooks very quickly over coals so keep a watchful eye on the progress. Serves 2-4. Go native with this entree, adding corn-on-the-cob, crusty seasoned bread and, for dessert, ice cream topped with a fresh berry sauce.

Fresh Berry Ice Cream Topping: Mash 1 cup blackberries. Combine with 1½ cups whole blackberries, ½ cup white sugar, 2 teaspoons cornstarch, 1 teaspoon grated lemon peel, ½ teaspoon cinnamon and ¼ teaspoon apple pie spice. Heat, stirring constantly, until thick and clear. Cool slightly. Serve over rich vanilla ice cream. Makes 2½-3 cups topping.

ITALIAN STYLE SMELT

2 pounds smelt, cleaned
1½ cups of your favorite or bottled spaghetti sauce
½ cup shredded mozzarella cheese

Distribute smelt evenly over the bottom of an oven dish. Pour sauce over smelt, sprinkle with cheese to cover, and bake at 400°F. for 10-15 minutes. Serves 4.

OVER-THE-WAVES DINING CHEF'S SPECIAL SOLE

5 ounces fresh fillet of Dover sole
2 ounces Dungeness crab meat
6 sliced ripe olives
2 ounces cream cheese
1 ounce dry sherry
2 teaspoons melted butter
1 quarter fresh lemon
3 tablespoons Hollandaise sauce
1 ounce Oregon baby shrimp
sprig parsley

Pat sole dry. Combine cream cheese, crab meat, ripe olives, and sherry. Roll mixture into sole. Place in casserole dish. Squeeze juice from lemon over sole plus 2 teaspoons butter.

Bake in 350°F. oven for 15 minutes. Remove, drain liquid from casserole, cover with Hollandaise sauce and baby shrimp, garnish with a sprig of parsley. Serves 1.

LA SERRE RICHLY STUFFED SOLE

1½ pounds fillet of sole
4 tablespoons finely chopped onions
3 tablespoons butter
1½ cups bread crumbs (preferably from French sourdough bread)
2 tablespoons finely chopped parsley
½ teaspoon marjoram
dash of sea salt
freshly grated pepper
1 cup yogurt, plain
2 cups cream (or, 1 cup cream and 1 cup white wine with dash of sherry)

Sauce

2 tablespoons butter
2 tablespoons flour

1 tablespoon chopped pimento
1 tablespoon chopped green pepper
½ cup yogurt

Sauté onions until clear in butter. Add crumbs, parsley, yogurt and seasonings. Mix well and spread over fillets. Roll up and fasten with toothpicks in shallow dish. Add cream and bake 25 minutes at 350 °F.. Drain juice from fish and return sole to oven to keep warm. Sauce: Make roux with butter and flour in saucepan, heat gradually and add milk drained off fillets. Stir vigorously over medium heat and add yogurt and herbs. Serve over fish. Sprinkle with pimentos and chopped peppers on top. Serves 4.

PORTSIDE FILET OF PETRALE NORMANDE

3¼ pounds petrale sole
1 pound fresh mussels
12 ounces mushrooms
12 small oysters
12 ounces shrimp meat
2 shallots
2 egg yolks
2 cups heavy cream
½ pint white wine
1 lemon
1 cup butter
6 croutons of bread
salt and white pepper

Poach the fillet of sole until tender in white wine and chopped shallots and use the stock to make a cream sauce using roux. Add heavy cream, ½ cup butter and egg yolks away from heat.

Sauté shrimp, mussels, mushrooms, oysters with ½ cup butter and white wine. Cook for three to five minutes. Add to the cream sauce, season with salt and white pepper. Allow ten minutes for cooking. My personal opinion would be to add one ounce of Calvados brandy. Serves 6.

ROD 'N REEL SHRIMP STUFFED SOLE

4 ribs of celery, including leaves
4 green onions
¼ pint mayonnaise
1 pound cooked cocktail shrimp
24 pieces fillet of sole, 8 inches in length (approximately 4 pounds)
¼ cup melted butter (½ of 1 stick)
¼ cup white wine (Rhine preferred)
¾ cup water
24 round toothpicks
3 lemons
parsley flakes
paprika

Chop celery and green onions, chopping celery finer than onions. Mix together in large mixing bowl.

Add mayonnaise and mix together until well blended. Add shrimp and mix gently so as not to break up the shrimp meat.

Place heaping tablespoons of mixture on each fillet of sole and roll up tightly, with pointed end of fish up. Secure with toothpick and place side by side on pan and dab with melted butter. Sprinkle with parsley flakes, paprika, and wine.

Add water and bake in 425 °F. oven 15-20 minutes. Since all ovens cook differently, you may need to cook it a little more. Makes 12 orders of 2 roll-ups per person.

If you are having just this entree without any courses before it, I would serve 3 roll-ups each and the recipe will serve 8 people.

FLOUNDER WITH SEAFOOD SAUCE

1-2 pounds flounder fillets
court bouillon (see Index)
½ cup Pineau des Charentes
2 egg yolks, beaten slightly
1 tablespoon cream
2 mushrooms, sliced
8 scallops, sliced

8 baby shrimp
1 tablespoon chopped parsley

Poach flounder in court bouillon. Remove fillets from liquid and divide among four individual serving dishes. Measure 1½ cups of court bouillon into saucepan. Add Pineau des Charentes and heat. Combine yolks and cream and slowly stir into the hot liquid. Continue heating, stirring constantly, until mixture thickens. Fold in mushrooms, scallops and shrimp, heating only until scallops are opaque. Divide among the four dishes, pouring over the fillets. Sprinkle with parsley and place under boiler until bubbly and golden in color. Serves 4. Dessert might be an attractive tray of seasonal fruits, various cheeses and crackers.

RIVER SEA INN MAHI MAHI

Skin and portion fish. Season with salt and white pepper. Dip lightly in flour. Melt 2 ounces butter in skillet; saute Mahi Mahi slowly until golden brown and well done. Put on serving plate and keep warm.

Garnish Topping

Peel and chunk fresh pineapple. Melt 2 ounces butter in skillet and saute lightly until warm; add a dash of brown sugar and a dash of white wine. Pour approximately 4 ounces of chunks over each fish portion and sprinkle with sliced almonds and shredded coconut. Place under broiler or in hot oven until brown.

HALIBUT KEBABS

1 pound halibut, cut into 1" squares
⅓ cup oil
1 tablespoon lime juice
¼ teaspoon powdered garlic
½ teaspoon basil
½ teaspoon thyme leaves
green onions
parboiled onions
mushrooms
bay leaves
cherry tomatoes
lime wedges

Combine oil, lime juice, garlic powder, basil and thyme leaves. Add halibut and stir gently to coat completely. Cover and marinate overnight. Drain halibut, reserving marinade. Insert fish squares on skewers, alternating with onions, mushrooms, bay leaves, and tomatoes. Brushing occasionally with reserved liquid, broil or grill until fish is opaque. Serves 2-4 with lime wedges on the side to allow diners to further highlight the entree. Here's an idea: next time, why not set out dishes of the kebab ingredients and let your guests put together their own party kebabs!

Shellfish

. . . . GEODUCKS . . . .

Rinse the live geoduck under cold, running water. Using a very sharp knife, insert and run around the shell, freeing body from shell. Discard shell.

Cut siphon away from body. Pour boiling water over siphon, loosening the skin. Pull back and discard the skin. Split siphon and grind or pound to tenderize. Using knife, cut the stomach membrane away from the skin-covered mantle, freeing the stomach. Discard membrane.

Split stomach and discard interior dark parts. Split mantle along crease; pour boiling water over it to loosen skin. Pull back and discard skin.

Slice both mantle and stomach pieces and use as is, since they are both very tender. A 2-to-3-pound geoduck serves 4.

STIR-FRIED GEODUCK WITH HAM AND ALMONDS

mantle and stomach from a 2-to-3-pound geoduck, cut in ¼″ slices
1½ tablespoons soy sauce
2 tablespoons sherry
1 teaspoon brown sugar
1 tablespoon cornstarch
½ cup slivered almonds
2 thin slices ginger root
½ cup ham cut into matchstick-sized pieces
¼ cup chicken broth
2 tablespoons oil

Marinate geoduck in mixture of soy sauce, sherry, brown sugar, and cornstarch for 10 minutes.

Meanwhile, heat 1 tablespoon oil and sauté almonds until golden brown. Set aside.

Heat remaining oil and sauté ginger root until oil is well flavored. Remove and discard ginger root.

Add geoduck mixture and ham. Stir fry 2-5 minutes, just until geoduck firms. Add chicken broth and cook 1 minute or until sauce thickens. Stir in almonds and serve 2-3.

GEODUCK IN WINE SAUCE

siphon from 2-to-3-pound geoduck, skinned, split, and pounded to tenderize
flour
3 tablespoons butter
1 tablespoon lemon juice
about ¼ cup white dinner wine

Melt butter in wide skillet. Cut geoduck into single-serving-size pieces and lightly flour.

Add to sizzling butter and slightly brown on both sides. Sprinkle lemon juice over geoduck and cook 1 minute longer.

Pour in wine and cook a few minutes longer, using just enough wine to make a sauce of proper consistency. Serves 2-3.

GEODUCK RANGOON

½ cup ground or chopped geoduck
4 ounces cream cheese
1 tablespoon snipped chives
2 teaspoons Worcestershire sauce
1 teaspoon paprika
2 dozen won ton skins

Combine geoduck, cream cheese, chives, Worcestershire sauce, and paprika.

Place drop of mixture off center on won ton skin; fold into triangle and bend edges up as shown in diagram.

Fry in oil preheated to 375°F. until skins are golden. Drain and serve 4-8.

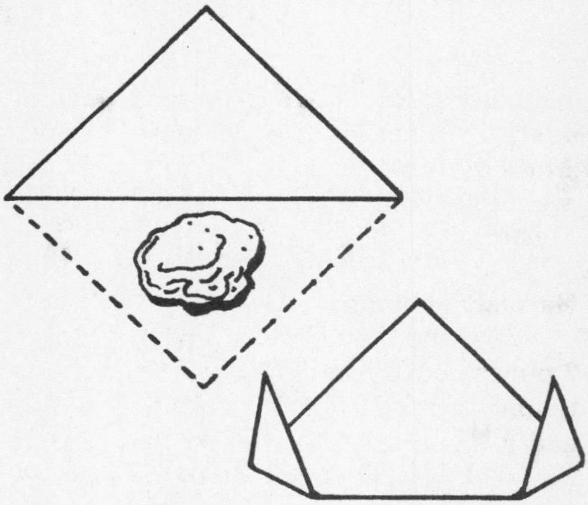

GEODUCK PICCATA

1 large geoduck
flour, salt and pepper
¼-½ cup butter
2-4 tablespoons oil
5 tablespoons water
5 tablespoons lemon juice
½ cup coarsely chopped walnuts
lemon slices

Prepare geoduck, cutting siphon into

4 pieces, pounding to tenderize, and slicing mantle. Dredge in mixture of flour and salt and pepper. Melt ¼ cup butter in large frying pan. Add walnuts and stir until golden and toasted. Remove to heated dish. Add 2 tablespoons oil to remaining butter. Quickly brown clam pieces, removing cooked portions to heated platter. Add more butter and oil as needed. When all meat is cooked and removed from pan, stir in water and lemon juice, being sure to scrape the pan thoroughly to loosen all particles. Boil until desired consistency. Pour sauce over the geoduck, sprinkle with nuts and garnish with lemon slices. Serves 2. For dessert, you might choose a refreshing tray of papaya halves, pineapple quarters and melon slices.

. . . . STEAMER CLAMS . . . .

Scrub under running water to remove most visible sand, discarding any dead clams.

Set in large bucket of salted water (about ½ cup salt to a bucket), and allow to set several hours in order for the clams to clean themselves.

Some cooks prefer to use a handful of cornmeal in addition to the salt. Figure on 1-1½ pounds of steamer clams per serving.

CLAMS WITH CORN AND HAM

2-3 pounds steamer clams, cleaned
2 tablespoons oil
2 onions, chopped
⅛ teaspoon powdered garlic
2 teaspoons paprika
8 ounces cooked ham, cut into cubes
¼ cup white dinner wine
1 bay leaf
⅛ teaspoon liquid hot pepper sauce
2 tomatoes, peeled and chopped
7½ ounces jar of baby corn-on-the-cob

Heat oil and cook onions until slightly browned. Stir in garlic and paprika. Add ham and cook until slightly browned. Stir in wine, bay leaf, hot pepper sauce, and tomatoes.

Bring to boil, lower heat, and simmer covered about 15 minutes. Add clams and corn, coating well with sauce. Cover and steam until clams open.

Serve as is in large soup bowls, or remove clams to heated platter and boil liquid until of sauce consistency and pour over clams. Serves 2.

STIR-FRIED CLAMS IN GARLIC BUTTER

5 pounds steamer clams, cleaned
½ cup butter
2 tablespoons finely chopped onion
1 clove garlic, finely chopped

Melt butter in large skillet; sauté onion and garlic until flavors are released. Stir in clams, drenching with butter mixture.

Cover pan and cook until clams open. Uncover and mix to bring sauce back over clams. Serve in wide-mouth bowls with sauce. Serves 4.

CLAMS IN BEER SAUCE

2-3 pounds steamer clams, cleaned
1 medium onion, cut in half and sliced
2 tablespoons oil
⅛ teaspoon powdered garlic
1 cup flat beer
2 tablespoons lemon juice
⅛ teaspoon cayenne pepper
⅛ teaspoon ground oregano

Heat oil and sauté onion until limp. Add garlic, beer, lemon juice, cayenne pepper, and oregano. Bring to boil and stir in clams, coating well with mixture.

Cover and steam until clams open. Remove clams to heated platter and boil down sauce until thickened. Pour over clams and serve 2 in wide soup bowls.

.... RAZOR CLAMS ....

Pour boiling water very quickly over live razor clams to open. Run knife between shell sides, cutting muscles. Slice off dark tip of neck and open body from end to end. Butterfly cutting is best.

Discard all dark parts including gills and digestive tract. Run knife along digger so it will lie flat. Rinse under cold, running water and drain well before cooking.

Razor clams may be used either whole or ground. Three to four razor clams make a generous serving.

PIXIE KITCHEN FAMOUS CLAM DIP

(As Printed in Ford Times)

8 ounces cream cheese
8 ounces minced clams
1 tablespoon mayonnaise
½ teaspoon garlic salt
1 tablespoon Worcestershire sauce
¼ teaspoon monosodium glutamante

Add clam juice for consistency desired and mix all the ingredients, then refrigerate. The secret to the success of this dip is to make it at least 4-7 days before serving, which allows all the flavors to blend.

WHOLE FRIED RAZOR CLAMS

Whole razor clams are at their choicest when prepared in abundance with a light, flavorful coating. Experiment and discover your tastiest selection from the ideas suggested here or create your own. Our personal favorite is crushed Ritz crackers.

Simply dip razor clam into mixture of egg and milk or egg cut with sherry, then into coating.

- **crushed crackers, such as Ritz, Chicken-in-a-Biskit**
- **cornmeal or cornmeal blended with flour**
- **flour with seasonings such as paprika or dill weed**
- **bread crumbs and flour mixture**
- **seasoned croutons that have been crushed in a blender**
- **sesame seeds blended with flour**
- **crushed corn or wheat cereal flakes**
- **pancake or biscuit mixes**

Fry coated clams quickly in very hot oil, turning once.

CLAM STUFFING FOR CHICKEN

1 cup ground or chopped clams
½ cup butter
½ cup chopped celery
½ cup chopped green onions
4 cups day old French bread cubes
2 tablespoons chopped parsley
½ teaspoon dried thyme leaves
½ teaspoon ground marjoram

Melt butter, add celery and green onions and sauté until golden. Remove from heat. Toss with remaining ingredients and stuff bird. Easily stuffs 5-pound bird to serve 4 people.

CLAMS IN HAM SAUCE

1 cup ground or chopped clams
¼ cup butter
½ pound mushrooms, sliced
½ cup sliced green onions
8 whole water chestnuts, diced

6 ounces ham, slivered
3 tablespoons flour
4 egg whites, beaten stiff

Heat butter and sauté green onions and mushrooms. Add water chestnuts, ham, clams, and flour and cook until thick. Spoon into 4 buttered individual baking shells or one large dish and cover with egg whites.

Bake in 400°F. oven until heated thoroughly and egg whites are lightly browned. Serves 4.

CRUNCHY CLAM FRITTERS

½ cup ground or chopped clams
½ cup flour
2 eggs, slightly beaten
4-6 ounces bean sprouts, lightly chopped
1 teaspoon baking powder
¼ teaspoon liquid hot pepper sauce
½ tablespoon soy sauce
2 green onions, sliced

Combine all ingredients and blend well. Drop by teaspoons into preheated 375°F. oil and fry until golden. Drain well on paper towels. Serve 2 with Worcestershire sauce.

CLAMS IN RED SAUCE

½ cup ground or chopped clams
6 ounces fine egg noodles, cooked
2 tablespoons butter
1 cup sliced mushrooms
1 small onion, chopped
⅓ cup thinly sliced celery
1 cup tomato catsup or sauce
3 ounces Colby cheese, grated

Melt butter and add mushrooms, onion and celery. Heat until lightly browned. Stir in clams and tomato catsup or sauce and heat until warmed thoroughly.

In a one-quart oven dish, alternate layers of cooked noodles, clam mixture, and grated cheese, ending with a sprinkling of cheese. Bake at 375°F. for 30 minutes or until cheese is melted and bubbly. Serves 2-3.

CLAM SOUFFLÉ

24 soda crackers
milk
2 eggs, well beaten
½ cup thinly sliced celery
½ cup butter, melted
½-1 cup minced clams
dash hot pepper sauce
paprika

Crumble crackers and cover with milk in baking dish. Combine eggs, celery, butter, clams, and hot pepper sauce in separate bowl. Pour over cracker mixture. Sprinkle with paprika. Bake 25 minutes at 350°F. Serves 4 as a luncheon dish. To complete the luncheon, try serving a hot, buttery French bread, crisp green and mushroom salad with Basil Dressing, and a chilled native Oregon dry white wine.

Basil Salad Dressing: Combine in shaker jar ½ cup oil, ¼ cup tarragon vinegar, 1 teaspoon each sugar and basil, ¼ teaspoon powdered garlic, ½ teaspoon salt, ¼ teaspoon lemon pepper and 1 tablespoon toasted sesame seeds. Shake until well blended and serve over salad greens. Makes about 1 cup dressing.

. . . . CRAB . . . .

Bring large pot of salted water (¼ cup salt to 1 quart water) to boil. Add pickling spices, if desired, to cut down on cooking odors.

Plunge live crab into water, upside down so legs will fold up against shell. Return pot to boil immediately so crab will die instantly. Lightly boil 15-20 minutes.

Remove crab and plunge into another pot of water, this one cold, to stop the cooking process. Clean by lifting off top portion of shell and discarding along with yellow fat and gills on either side of the back. Turn crab over and break off mouth and tail. Scrape out center part and entrails. Break in half. Rinse fully under cold, running water.

A medium whole crab will satisfy 2 diners, while a pound of crab meat in sauce will provide 4-8 servings.

CRACKED CRAB WITH RICE VINEGAR

Present each diner with one-half of a whole, cleaned crab. Accompany with small bowl of sauce. Allow each person to shell his own crab and dip meat into either one of the sauces listed.

Sauce 1: Simply pour rice wine vinegar into small individual serving bowls for a tangy dipping sauce.

Sauce 2: Combine ½ cup rice wine vinegar, 2 tablespoons sherry, and 1 teaspoon minced ginger root. Pour into individual serving bowls.

CRAB BROILER CRAB AU GRATIN

1 quart milk
½ cup butter
⅓ cup flour
⅓ teaspoon dry mustard
dash cayenne pepper
⅓ quart ground nippy cheese
¼ cup sherry
½ teaspoon chicken base

Scald milk, Melt butter, add flour, mustard, and cayenne and blend. Add to scalded milk and cook about 8 minutes. Add cheese and wine and stir until melted and blended. Let cool. Makes 1½ quarts of sauce.

For individual Crab Au Gratin servings, use 8 ounce casserole. Pour 1½ ounces cheese sauce in bottom of dish. Mold 5 ounces Dungeness crab meat to size of dish. Pour 1½ ounces more of cheese sauce over the crab meat and then sprinkle grated nippy cheese over the sauce. Cook in 400°F. oven until ingredients become bubbly. If more browning is required, place under a broiler until the desired color is obtained. Do not burn.

Garnish with several large crab legs, ground parsley, and paprika. Place 2 large olives (black) on top for additional garnish. Toast points can also be placed on top.

THE WHALER'S CRAB LEGS À LA LAROUSSE

2½ cups crab legs
⅛ cup melted butter
⅛ cup chablis wine
¾ cup sliced mushrooms
½ tomato cut in wedges
4 ripe olives
4 green olives

Sauté above ingredients over medium heat for about 5 minutes. Pour into 2 serving dishes and devour.

LA SERRE CRAB CREPES

½ cup unsalted butter
¼ cup fresh minced parsley
⅛ teaspoon crushed elephant garlic
1 pound fresh mushrooms, thinly sliced
⅔ cup sherry
1 pint heavy cream
1 tablespoon arrowroot powder
1 pound freshly picked crab

In a heavy skillet, melt the butter and add the parsley, garlic, mushrooms, and sherry and stir until mushrooms are slightly limp. Add the cream and arrowroot powder. Continue to stir over low heat until desired thickness, add more cream or milk accordingly. Add lastly the crab and fold into sauce. This can be used with crepes and topped with a mild cheese sauce or served over rice and topped with grated jack cheese and placed in oven until cheese is melted and bubbly.

Whole Wheat Crepes

In a blender or food processor combine: 3 eggs and ⅔ cup of whole wheat pastry flour. Gradually add 1 cup milk and ¼ cup Curacao liqueur. Blend until smooth and creamy. Use 6" crepe pan. Makes 10 to 16 crepes.

THE WINDWARD INN MUSHROOM CAPS STUFFED WITH DUNGENESS CRABMEAT

18-24 large mushrooms
lemon juice
2 tablespoons butter
1 tablespoon dry sherry
4 thick slices bacon
½ of a small onion—minced
8-10 individual saltine crackers crumbled
8 ounces cooked crabmeat
2 ounces grated Swiss cheese
2 ounces grated cheddar cheese
salt and pepper

Clean mushrooms by wiping with a paper towel moistened with lemon juice. Remove the stem from the caps and set the caps aside. Mince the stems and saute them gently in the butter adding the dry sherry about 2 minutes before removing from heat. Set aside.

Fry the bacon medium crisp and drain on a paper towel. Sauté the minced onion in the bacon grease. Mince the bacon.

Combine the mushroom stems, onion and bacon. Add the crabmeat and the cracker crumbs. Mix well. If the mixture is dry, moisten with more dry sherry. If mixture is too moist, add more cracker crumbs. Salt and pepper to taste.

Stuff the mushroom caps with the crab mixture and top with a pinch of each of the grated cheeses.

Place the mushroom caps on a lightly buttered baking sheet and put under the broiler 4-5 minutes until the cheese is melted, bubbling, and lightly browned. Serves 4 as an entree.

ORIENTAL CRAB DIP

½ pound crab meat
½ cup chopped water chestnuts
2 tablespoons sliced green onions
2 tablespoons soy sauce
½ cup mayonnaise or ¼ cup mayonnaise with ¼ cup sour cream

Combine all ingredients and serve immediately with rice crackers. Serves 4-6.

CRAB FONDUE

1 pound crab meat
10 ounce jar cheddar cheese spread
16 ounces cream cheese
¼ cup milk
1 teaspoon Worcestershire sauce
dash liquid hot pepper sauce
¼ cup flat beer
bread cubes and/or large, cooked and shelled shrimp

Melt cheeses over boiling water. Add crab meat, milk, Worcestershire sauce, hot pepper sauce, and beer. Heat until warmed through and serve in fondue pot accompanied with bread cubes and/or shrimp for dipping. Serves 4.

CRAB SANDWICHES

½ pound crab meat
1 egg yolk
5 ounces processed American

cheese spread
1 teaspoon Worcestershire sauce
¼ teaspoon onion powder
cocktail rye bread, buttered

Combine cheese spread and egg yolk. Blend in crab meat, Worcestershire sauce, and onion powder. Spread on buttered bread slices and place in 400°F. oven until lightly browned. Serves 3-6.

CRAB & AVOCADO CASSEROLE

½ pound crab meat
1 cup evaporated milk
2 tablespoons butter
2 tablespoons flour
4 tablespoons lemon juice
2 large avocados, peeled and diced
1 teaspoon drained capers

Toss avocados with lemon juice and set aside. Melt butter and blend in flour. Stir in milk slowly and heat until thickened. Add crab meat, avocados, and capers.

Divide among 4 lightly buttered individual baking shells or casserole dish and bake at 375°F. until very hot, about 20-25 minutes. Serves 4.

BRANDIED CRAB

1 pound crab meat
4 tablespoons butter
1 onion, finely chopped
¼ pound mushrooms, sliced
2 tablespoons chopped parsley
½ teaspoon curry powder
3 tablespoons tomato-based seafood sauce
1 tablespoon brandy
¼ teaspoon liquid hot pepper sauce
¼ cup sherry
½ cup whipping cream
1½ cups bread crumbs tossed with 2 tablespoons melted butter and 1 tablespoon chopped parsley

Melt butter in frying pan and sauté onions and mushrooms until moisture is released. Stir in parsley, curry, seafood sauce, brandy, hot pepper sauce, sherry, and whipping cream. Remove from heat and fold in crab.

Divide among 4 individual baking shells and top each with layer of crumbs. Bake at 400°F. for 12 minutes or until crumbs are golden. Serves 4.

GRILLED KING CRAB LEGS

1 pound king crab legs, thawed and shelled
⅓ cup melted butter
2 tablespoons snipped chives
. ¼ cup lemon juice

Combine butter, chives and lemon juice. Pat onto crab legs. Place crab legs over medium coals, brushing and turning as necessary until heated throughout. Serves 2-3. Great party dish, allowing guests to prepare and grill their own selection. Corn-on-the-cob is a nice addition to this menu and Creme de Menthe parfaits are a grand finale.

Creme de Menthe Parfaits: Layer rich vanilla ice cream with dribblings of Creme de Menthe liqueur, whipped cream and toasted slivered almonds. Top with stemmed maraschino cherry.

. . . . CRAYFISH . . . .

No special preparation is required for crayfish; the live crayfish are quickly dropped into boiling stock, as detailed in the following recipe, and lifted out when a bright pink color. Usually only the tail portion is consumed, although the claws do hold a tiny, tender piece of meat.

CRAYFISH STOCK POT

live crayfish
5 quarts water
2 cups white dinner wine
2 large onions, quartered
3 large carrots, sliced
1 whole lemon, sliced
10 whole black peppercorns
5 whole allspice
2 whole bay leaves
2 teaspoons salt

Combine all ingredients except crayfish and bring to boil. Add live crayfish, one at a time, head first to kill instantly.

Bring liquid back to boil and simmer a few minutes until crayfish are a bright red color. Remove from pot and drain.

Eat as soon as cool enough to handle, accompanied by bowls of melted butter for dipping, crusty French rolls, and a fine dry white wine.

ADDITIONAL SUGGESTIONS FOR SERVING CRAYFISH

Crayfish freeze quite successfully when first cooked in stockpot, allowed to cool, placed in freezer container, and covered with cooled stock. When ready to use, thaw the resulting block of ice in a strainer and use crayfish in any number of ways, as suggested by the following:

- Add as finishing touch to seafood soups such as bouillabaisse.
- Place on iced seafood platter and surround with lemon and lime slices as party hors d'oeuvres.
- Accompany Crayfish with small bowls of dips such as homemade mayonnaise and dill flavored dips for an informal first course to festive dinner.

.... LOBSTER ....

When selecting your lobster, look for one whose tail curls under when picked up. If lobster is already cooked, be sure that the tail is curled, indicating it was alive when cooked. Lobster may be successfully prepared by either boiling or broiling, although most "gourmets" prefer boiling. One-pound whole lobster or an 8-ounce tail serves 1.

To Boil. Bring salted fresh water or sea water to boil, plunge lobster head first into water, return to boil, timing 5 minutes for first pound and 3 minutes for each pound thereafter. Remove from cooking water and clean. Cut off small portion of head, allowing body liquid to drain. Either cut shell in half or split with mallet. Remove and discard black vein running along tail as well as stomach sac behind the eyes. The female's "coral" or roe and the green liver of both sexes are considered fine eating. Stir into the bowl of melted butter used for dipping the lobster in.

To Broil. Using a sharp knife, cut deeply where body and head meet, severing spinal cord and immediately killing lobster. Cut the length of the lobster or use mallet, drain, remove vein and stomach. Brush with melted butter and set flesh side up in oven to broil 5 inches away from heat source for 10-15 minutes; baste frequently with butter.

MANNI'S HILLTOP HOUSE LOBSTER THERMIDOR

1 lobster tail, approximately 1 pound
2 tablespoons chopped onions
2 tablespoons chopped green pepper
2 tablespoons chopped mushrooms
1 tablespoon chopped pimentos
pinch of salt

1 tablespoon drawn butter
2½ cups basic white cream sauce
3 tablespoons straight sherry
cheddar cheese
lemon star

Sauté vegetables in drawn butter for about 2 minutes. Clean lobster meat from tail. Chop lobster meat coarsely and add to the sauteed vegetables. Then add basic cream sauce, salt, sherry and cook for approximately 5 minutes. Then take clean split lobster tail and pour sauce into the shell, top with cheddar cheese and bake until melted. Garnish with lemon star. Serves 1-2.

GRILLED LOBSTER-BACON WRAPS

½ pound cooked lobster meat, cut into bite-sized pieces
⅓ cup soy sauce
1 teaspoon sugar
⅛ teaspoon red pepper flakes
1 8-ounce can water chestnuts, drained
bacon strips, cut into halves

Combine soy sauce, sugar and red pepper flakes in small bowl. Gently stir in lobster pieces. Drain. Roll up lobster piece and water chestnut in bacon strip, securing with toothpick. Arrange on oven sheet and place in 350°F. oven for 8-10 minutes to reduce fat. Remove and place over medium coals until bacon is crisp and golden. Pour a chilled sauterne, and you'll keep guests talking long after the party's over with this very special appetizer.

BARBECUED ROCK LOBSTER

2 medium rock lobster tails, butterflied
¼ cup melted butter
1 teaspoon lemon juice
½ teaspoon lemon peel
1 tablespoon brandy
½ teaspoon anise seed

Combine butter, lemon juice and peel, brandy, and anise seed. Brush lobster with this mixture and place on grill with the meat side up. Turn after about five minutes, brushing with butter mixture occasionally, and grilling until lobster is opaque. Serves 2. Any white dinner wine would be appreciated here but champagne is always perfect to dress up an outdoor dinner. Complete the evening with Coffee Galliano.

Coffee Galliano: Fold ⅓ cup Liquore Galliano into 1 cup whipped cream. Spoon mixture gently onto the top of 6 cups of strong coffee and serve.

LOBSTER COCKTAIL

1 pound lobster meat, cubed
lemon wedges
Homemade Cocktail Sauce

Divide lobster among 4 cocktail glasses, top with Homemade Cocktail Sauce, garnish with lemon wedges. Serve to 4 along with crusty rolls and butter.

Homemade Cocktail Sauce: Combine 1 cup prepared chili sauce, ⅓ cup lemon juice, 1 teaspoon lime juice, 2 teaspoons finely chopped onions, 2 teaspoons Worcestershire sauce, and 3 dashes hot pepper sauce. Chill thoroughly.

LOBSTER SPREAD

1 cup cooked lobster meat
⅓ cup sour cream
4 tablespoons Madeira
1 tablespoon chopped chives

Combine the lobster meat, sour cream and Madeira in a blender, whirling until well blended. Place in serving bowl or crock and sprinkle with chives. Chill well and serve as appetizer surrounded with simple crackers or toast rounds. A real treat when accompanied with a bottle of chilled champagne.

LOBSTER BISQUE

½ pound cooked lobster meat, sliced thin
1 cup cream
1 cup clam juice
½ teaspoon dill seed
1 tablespoon butter
1 teaspoon cornstarch
1 tablespoon water
chopped parsley

Combine cream and clam juice in saucepan. Heat gently until very warm. Add dill seed, butter and lobster meat. Combine cornstarch and water and stir in mixture. Heat 15 minutes or until slightly thickened and very warm, being careful not to boil. Serves 2-4, sprinkling individual bowls with parsley. A rich dish, be sure to follow with simple entree such as grilled steak and fresh asparagus spears.

. . . . MUSSELS . . . .

Most of the mussel's dirt is on the outside, so no soaking is necessary as is for the steamer clams. Simply scrub the mussel's shell with rough brush under running water, discarding any that are not alive. Trim beard (that bundle of fine brown threads) with scissors and prepare, planning on 1-1½ pounds mussels per serving.

Special caution should be exercised if collecting your own mussels. Take only during safe months, usually November 1 through March 31. Check with State Department of Fisheries if you are uncertain when safe period is. During the late summer months mussels can absorb a highly toxic form of algae leading to sickness and sometimes even death in the consumer.

GARLICKY MUSSEL HORS D'OEUVRES

2 pounds of mussels, lightly steamed, just to open
½ cup butter, softened
2 slices bacon, well minced
1 tablespoon snipped chives
⅜ teaspoon powdered garlic
1 tablespoon lemon juice

Prepare mussels by discarding one-half of the shell and setting mussel in center of retained shell. Blend butter, bacon, chives, garlic, and lemon juice. Place a dab of butter mixture on top of each mussel.

Set shells on a shallow baking pan and bake at 400°F. until bubbling, about 5-10 minutes. Serves 8-12.

THE WINDWARD INN SEA MUSSELS MARINIERS

7 dozen (approximately 4 pounds) fresh mussels in the shell
4 tablespoons butter
4 cloves garlic—minced
1 medium sweet onion—chopped fine
juice of ½ lemon
2 cups dry white wine
¼ cup chopped parsley

In a large soup pot melt the butter and add the onion and garlic. Sauté lightly but do not brown. Add the lemon juice and wine and bring to a boil. Add the mussels and stir to mix with the other ingredients. Cover and boil for 5 minutes or until the shells open. Another stir about half-way through the cooking will ensure that they cook evenly.

Serve the mussels in wide soup bowls and ladle the broth over them. Garnish with chopped parsley. Provide crusty French bread for sopping up the broth and a chilled light, dry white wine for washing everything down. Serves 4 as an entree.

.... OCTOPUS ....

Prepare raw octopus by slitting the head cavity open and removing interior portion. Cut out the beak. Drop octopus into rapidly boiling water, spreading legs. Check to be sure octopus is completely covered by the water, lower heat, and cook one-half hour. Remove from water, cut off suction cups if large, peel back skin and slice.

If octopus has already been cooked, cut off suction cups, peel back skin and slice ready to eat. Smaller octopus tend to be more tender; however large octopus may be pounded to produce a more tender product. 4-8 ounces of octopus in sauce will serve 2.

OCTOPUS IN PERNOD SAUCE

4 ounces octopus slices
3 tablespoons butter
1 tablespoon flour
½ cup chicken broth diluted with
¼ cup water
¼ teaspoon whole tarragon leaves
1 tablespoon Pernod

Melt 2 tablespoons butter and stir in flour. Cook until bubbly. Slowly add chicken broth mixture and cook until thickened. Stir in tarragon.

In another pan, melt remaining butter and very lightly stir-fry octopus slices to heat. Add Pernod and flame. Stir sauce into octopus mixture and serve 2.

JAPANESE OCTOPUS

Slice octopus on the diagonal. Arrange on a platter and accompany with bowl of Shiro Miso for dipping. Shiro Miso, easily obtainable at any Oriental market, is a light-gray-colored paste made from soy beans that will lend a slightly sweet flavor to this delicacy.

OCTOPUS DIP

1 cup ground octopus
½ carton tofu (whirl in blender until smooth), or 2 cups sour cream, yogurt or a mixture of these
½ teaspoon powdered garlic
2 tablespoons lemon juice
2 tablespoons finely chopped onions
2 tablespoons chopped chives

Combine all ingredients and serve with vegetables for dipping. Makes about 3 cups. Suggested vegetables: cauliflower, red and green pepper squares, potato wafers, celery and carrot sticks, squash and cucumber slices.

OCTOPUS CHOWDER

1 cup coarsely ground octopus
2 tablespoons butter
4 slices bacon, chopped
½ cup chopped onions
1 cup diced potato
¼ cup chopped celery
2 cups chicken broth
1 pound can stewed tomatoes
½ teaspoon thyme
1 tablespoon Worcestershire sauce
¼ teaspoon hot pepper sauce
chopped parsley

Sauté bacon and onions in melted butter. Add potato, celery and chicken broth. Cover and simmer until potato is tender. Add tomatoes, thyme, Worcestershire sauce, hot pepper sauce and octopus and simmer uncovered 30 minutes. Serves 4-6 with parsley sprinkled in individual serving bowls. Add rolls or bread and a fresh green salad for a satisfying lunch or light dinner.

MARINATED OCTOPUS

Octopus tentacle, cooked and sliced ¼" thick
Vinegar and oil salad dressing, either homemade or prepared
French bread

Cover octopus slices with well-seasoned salad dressing. Marinate several days. Drain and serve with French bread as appetizer. This dish is best when contrasted by simpler finger foods. Consider serving along with cucumber rounds, carrot curls, celery fans, etc.

. . . . OYSTERS . . . .

Scrub well under running water with stiff brush, discarding any that are open as these are dead. Insert knife or screwdriver into hinged part of oyster and push so as to sever muscle. Run along remainder of shell. Lift off shallow half of shell and loosen oyster from shell. Pick over oysters to remove any pieces of shell.

If you prefer, oysters may also be slightly steamed or placed in a warmed oven to open more easily. ½ to ¾ cup shucked oysters or 3-4 whole medium oysters will serve 1 diner.

THE WINDWARD INN'S OYSTERS ROCKEFELLER

It is claimed that the original recipe for Oysters Rockefeller was invented in the late 1800's by Antoine's Restaurant in New Orleans and was derived from a snail dish that originated in Burgundy.

This recipe may seem a bit tedious, but the result is a superb dish that makes an outstanding entree or unusual hors d'oeuvre.

28-32 fresh small oysters in the shell
stiff brush
oyster knife
heavy saucepan

Shuck oysters and drop from shell with juice into heavy saucepan. Save deep half of shell and scrub to remove any sand.

2 tablespoons butter
juice of ½ lemon
¼ cup dry white wine

Add butter, lemon juice, and white wine to saucepan with oysters. Bring to a gentle simmer for 2-3 minutes until oysters are just starting to get firm. Remove oysters from the cooking juice and set them aside.

¼ cup dry white wine
1 teaspoon absinthe or pernod
cheesecloth

Add the additional wine and the absinthe or pernod to the cooking juices and boil down rapidly until reduced by one-half. Now strain reduced juices through a piece of cheesecloth and set aside. (You should have approximately ½-¾ cup of strained liquid.)

3 tablespoons butter
2 tablespoons flour
½ cup light cream
heavy saucepan
wire whisk

Melt butter and stir in flour; let mixture bubble for 2-3 minutes, stirring constantly to make a light roux. Do not brown. Remove from heat. Stir in the strained oyster juice and beat with a wire whisk until smooth.

Back on the heat, slowly stir in cream and bring to a good simmer, stirring constantly. You should have approximately 1 cup medium consistency white sauce. Set aside.

1 cup cooked, finely minced spinach (Use fresh or frozen spinach; after cooking, press out all liquid and mince very fine)
2 tablespoons finely minced onion
½ teaspoon nutmeg

¼ teaspoon white pepper or cayenne
dash of salt
5 tablespoons butter
3 tablespoons fine, dry bread crumbs
heavy skillet

Sauté onion in 3 tablespoons of butter until soft. Add the other 2 tablespoons butter, spinach, nutmeg, salt, pepper, and bread crumbs. Gently sauté and blend the mixture for 2-3 minutes.

FINAL ASSEMBLY

the oyster shells
the spinach mixture
the oysters
the white sauce
¼ cup grated Parmesan cheese
4 slices bacon, cooked but not crisp, cut into 1-inch pieces

Place a spoonful of spinach mixture in each oyster shell and then an oyster. Spoon white sauce over oyster and spinach. Sprinkle on the Parmesan cheese and place a bacon piece on top.

You may prepare your Oysters Rockefeller ahead to this point and refrigerate.

TO SERVE

Place oysters in baking dish or pan (on bed of rock salt, if possible); put under a hot broiler for 2-4 minutes until bubbly and starting to brown. Garnish with lemon wedges and serve to 4.

THE ADOBE SCALLOPED OYSTERS

1 pint of fresh small oysters
1 pound of Saltine crackers
(2 packages from 1 pound box)
1 pint of half and half cream
¼ pound of butter

Break up crackers and mix with melted butter. Brown lightly in oven. Cut oysters into halves or quarters. Put into baking (serving) dish—one layer of oysters—one layer of crackers. Alternate with the remaining oysters and crackers. Cover oysters and crackers with half and half cream. Bake at 350°F. for 30 minutes. Serves 4.

OVER-THE-WAVES DINING OYSTER SAUTÉ

12 oysters
½ cup flour
3 tablespoons butter
½ ounce dry sherry
⅛ teaspoon ground sweet basil
dash of garlic salt
¼ cup diced (cooked) tomato
¼ cup chopped mushrooms
¼ cup finely chopped celery
2 green onions, chopped

In sauté pan, melt butter over medium heat. Lightly flour oysters and add to butter. Let oysters brown on underside. Add celery and sherry. Turn oysters over. Add garlic salt, basil, tomato, mushrooms and green onions. Continue to cook until oysters are done to your liking. Serves 2.

BEULAH'S SEA VIEW INN OYSTERS ST. CHARLES

1 cup chopped celery
1 cup chopped green pepper
½ cup chopped onions

Cook this in a small amount of water while preparing the following:

1 teaspoon salt
dash pepper
1 pint canned milk
6 tablespoons flour
6 tablespoons butter
¼ cup sherry
2 teaspoons Worcestershire sauce
1 pint small oysters, approximately
patty shells or toast points

Melt butter in pan, add flour and blend. Add milk and the rest of the ingredients, except the oysters, and cook until thick.

Sauté oysters in butter until they curl. Combine vegetables, oysters, and white sauce, serve in patty shells or toast points. Crab may be used, using about ½ cup for a serving.

Put in a buttered casserole, top with buttered crumbs, and bake in a 400°F. oven for about 15 minutes.

OYSTERS WITH ALMONDS ON THE HALF SHELL

6 medium oysters, removed from shell
the deeper side of the shell from each of the 6 oysters
2 tablespoons vinegar
1 tablespoon soy sauce
1 tablespoon retained oyster liquid
3½ ounces slivered almonds, chopped
2 slices bacon

Combine vinegar, soy sauce, and oyster liquid; marinate oysters in this mixture for 10-15 minutes. Remove from liquid and roll in nuts. Place each oyster back into its shell and cover oyster with ⅓ of a slice of bacon.

Set shells on a large baking sheet and place 8 inches under the oven's broiler. Broil 5 minutes or until bacon is crisp and oysters have started to curl around the edge. Serves 2.

OYSTER-SAUSAGE HORS D'OEUVRES

4 medium oysters, shucked and chopped fine
¼ pound sausage meat
⅛ teaspoon hot liquid pepper sauce
1 green onion, sliced
fine bread crumbs
tomato-based seafood sauce and chili sauce for dipping

Combine drained and chopped oysters, sausage, pepper sauce, green onion, and ½ cup fine bread crumbs. Form into balls and roll in bread crumbs to coat well.

Drop into oil preheated to 375°F. and fry until crumbs are golden brown. Drain and serve 4 accompanied with sauces for dipping.

OYSTERS LA PLAZA

24 oysters in the shell
1 pound medium cheddar cheese
1 No. 300 can asparagus spears
½ pound ground chorizo sausage
2 cups Spanish Sauce

SPANISH SAUCE

¼ cup chopped onion
2 tablespoons chopped green pepper
¼ cup chopped green chilies
1 No. 300 can diced tomatoes
dash of garlic
½ teaspoon chili powder
¼ teaspoon pepper
dash MSG
¼ teaspoon salt
1 tablespoon olive oil

Shuck oysters from shell, refrigerate oysters while preparing remaining ingredients. Clean oyster shells. An automatic dishwasher works very well for this. Allow shells to run several cycles. The extra shells should be saved so that you can prepare this recipe again by purchasing the raw oysters only.

Prepare Spanish Sauce by sautéeing onions, green pepper, and green chilies in olive oil. In a saucepan, combine remaining ingredients. Add sautéed vegetables and simmer for 20-30 minutes.

On a cookie sheet or oven-proof cookware, arrange cleaned oyster shells. Place in each oyster shell 1 teaspoon asparagus cut in ¼ inch pieces. On top of this place 1 teaspoon ground chorizo sausage. Place one oyster on top of this filling. Cover oyster with 1 teaspoon Spanish Sauce and top with sliced cheddar cheese, making slices approximately the same size as the oyster shell.

Place in 400°F. oven for 30 minutes, checking to see if cheese is bubbling. Serves 4 people. Dish may be prepared ahead, refrigerated, and cooked just before serving.

OYSTERS IN WINE SAUCE

6 medium oysters, removed from shell
the deeper side of the shell from each of the 6 oysters
¾ cup white dinner wine
2 tablespoons butter
2 tablespoons flour
⅓ cup light cream
1 tablespoon snipped chives
⅛ teaspoon liquid hot pepper sauce
2 tablespoons bread crumbs mixed with ½ teaspoon paprika and 1 tablespoon melted butter

Bring wine to boiling point. Lower heat and poach oysters lightly, about 1 minute. Remove and set back into their individual shells. Place on a large baking sheet and set aside.

Prepare sauce by melting butter in saucepan and stirring in flour. Cook until bubbly. Slowly blend in poaching wine and cream. Stir in chives and liquid hot pepper sauce. Cook until thickened. Spoon sauce over oysters and top evenly with crumbs.

Bake in 450°F. oven for 8-12 minutes or until crumbs are lightly toasted. Serves 2.

. . . . SCALLOPS . . . .

Normally scallops are to be found only in their ready-to-prepare stage. If, however, you should come across them in their shells, insert a sharp knife into the shell, freeing the muscle on both sides of the shell. Rinse under cold, running water and dry. Usually only the muscle is used, although the entire scallop is edible. One pound of scallops serves 2-3.

SCALLOPS WITH WINE OR SHERRY

1 pound scallops
½ cup oil
½ cup white dinner wine or sherry
½ cup soy sauce
½-1 teaspoon minced ginger root
⅛ teaspoon powdered garlic

Combine all ingredients and marinate scallops several hours. Remove from marinade, thread on skewers and broil 5-10 minutes, turning once and basting frequently. Serves 3-4.

PUFFY SCALLOP HORS D'OEUVRE

1 pound scallops, lightly poached in water and cooled
⅓ cup mayonnaise or sour cream
1 tablespoon sweet pickle relish
2 teaspoons lemon juice
2 teaspoons snipped chives
⅛-¼ teaspoon liquid hot pepper sauce
1 large egg white, beaten stiff

Combine mayonnaise or sour cream with pickle relish, lemon juice, chives, and hot pepper sauce. Gently fold in egg white.

Spread scallops on large shallow baking pan; top each scallop with drop of egg white mixture and broil until bubbly and brown. Serves 4-8.

SCALLOPS IN BOURBON SAUCE

2 pounds scallops
4 tablespoons butter

½ cup bourbon, warmed
¾ cup whipping cream
¾ cup retained scallop juices or bottled clam juice
flour

Melt butter in frying pan. Lightly flour scallops and sauté until golden brown. Remove to heated platter.

Pour in bourbon and very carefully flame. Stir in whipping cream and juice and boil down until proper consistency for sauce. Pour over scallops and serve 4-6.

SCALLOPS IN HONEY SAUCE

1 pound scallops
1 tablespoon honey
1 tablespoon prepared mustard
½ teaspoon curry powder
⅛ teaspoon powdered garlic

Combine honey, mustard, curry powder, and garlic powder. Warm until thin and smooth. Thread scallops on skewers and brush with sauce. Broil until translucent. Serves 3-4.

SCALLOPS IN RUM BUTTER

1 pound scallops
½ cup butter
⅛ teaspoon powdered garlic
1 tablespoon lemon juice
½ cup rum

Melt butter and stir in garlic and scallops. Sauté until translucent. Sprinkle with lemon juice. Pour in rum and flame.

Remove scallops to heated platter and boil sauce down to a proper consistency. Pour over scallops to serve 3-4.

. . . . SHRIMP . . . .

Shrimp may be shelled either before or after cooking. Grasp tail in left hand, slip right hand under feelers, and lift off several segments of shell. Holding firmly onto the tail, pull shrimp out of the shell.

Shrimp may be deveined before preparing, although this is primarily cosmetic, by making a shallow slit along the shrimp's curve and lifting out the black vein.

Cook the raw (green) shrimp by dropping into boiling salted water (¼ cup salt in 1 quart water) and simmering 2-5 minutes or until the shrimp are a bright pink color. For variety, parsley, onions, celery, and peppercorns may also be added to the cooking broth.

Butterfly shrimp by shelling and deveining green shrimp, being sure to leave the tail section on. Split along the back curve, cutting deep, almost to the shrimp's inner edge. Open and press flat.

One pound of green shrimp when cooked and shelled will give 1⅓-1⅔ cups meat (½ pound); makes 2 servings.

HADLEY HOUSE CREPES WITH SHRIMP

Crepe Batter: Whirl in blender or beat together in bowl.

1 cup water
1 cup milk
4 eggs
¼ cup melted margarine or oil
1 teaspoon salt
2 teaspoons sugar
2 cups flour

Cook on lightly greased hot griddle or in crepe pan, using ¼ cup batter per crepe. Yield: 16.

Filling: Make a thick sauce in double boiler or heavy pan.

¼ cup butter or margarine, melted

¼ cup chopped onion, sauteed in above
⅓ cup flour
3 cups milk
¼ teaspoon tarragon leaves
1 tablespoon sherry
½ cup grated Swiss cheese
salt and pepper to taste

Add about 1 cup of sauce to 3 cups cooked shrimp that have been sprinkled with lemon juice. Place 2 heaping tablespoons of shrimp filling on each crepe. Roll up and place in baking pan. Thin remaining sauce with milk if necessary and pour over crepes. Bake at 350°F. until sauce is bubbly and delicately browned. Yield: 6-8 servings.

OVER-THE-WAVES DINING CURRIED SHRIMP

¼ cup diced onions
¼ cup diced tomatoes
½ cup sliced mushrooms
2 tablespoons butter
1 teaspoon lemon juice
¼ cup dry sherry
2 teaspoons curry powder
3 cups baby shrimp meat
3 cups cooked white rice
chopped parsley
cornstarch

Sauté onions, mushrooms, tomatoes in butter. Add sherry, lemon juice, and curry powder. Bring to boil and thicken slightly with cornstarch. Add shrimp meat and warm gently.

Serve on bed of rice with chopped parsley sprinkled over top. Serves 4.

BLUE CHEESE-SHRIMP BUTTER

2-7½ ounce cans of cocktail shrimp, well drained
¾ pound butter
4 ounce package blue cheese
4 tablespoons sliced green onions

Beat butter with electric mixer until fluffy. Add cheese and beat again until fluffy. Fold in shrimp and onions. Use as a baked potato topping, accompanying grilled meats. Or, as a spread for hearty cocktail bread or thinly sliced brown bread. Or, on steamed broccoli for that special dinner party.

SEA HAG DON GRINDSTAFF'S BAKED STUFFED PRAWNS

1 pound (16/20) raw prawns, shelled, deveined and butterflied
½ pound butter
1 clove fresh garlic, chopped fine
4-6 ounces each crab and shrimp meat
¼ cup celery, chopped very fine
1 tablespoon diced sweet red pepper
1 tablespoon chives, diced very fine
1 teaspoon fine ground fresh bread crumbs
1 lemon wedge—the juice of
2 tablespoons mayonnaise
dash mace, salt and pepper

Melt the butter with the clove of garlic and allow to cool and sit approximately 15 minutes. Add the butterflied prawns to the garlic butter and marinate during preparation of the following. Combine the crab and shrimp meat with the celery, red pepper, chives, bread crumbs, lemon juice, mayonnaise and seasonings. Mix well. Select a suitable baking pan and arrange the marinated prawns—shell side down—flattened as much as possible. Place approximately 1 tablespoon of the stuffing mixture on each prawn, slightly molded and flattened to the shape and contour of the prawn. Cook the stuffed prawns in a 400°F. oven approximately 6-8 minutes or until the prawns are firm and the stuffing is hot. Serve the prawns as they are or top with fresh hollandaise or caper sauce. Serves 4.

SEA HAG
DON GRINDSTAFF'S
SHRIMP CURRY

½ cup butter
4 large onions, chopped in ½" pieces
3 cloves garlic, chopped fine
6 cups water
4 cups diced tomatoes
4 cups apples, peeled and diced in ½" pieces
2 cups celery, chopped in ½" pieces
½ cup shredded coconut
¾ teaspoon powdered ginger
1 tablespoon sugar
2 tablespoons curry powder
1½ tablespoons flour
1½ teaspoons seasoning salt
¼ teaspoon ground black pepper
1 pound 16/20 raw shrimp, shelled and deveined

Sauté the onion and garlic in the butter until lightly browned. Bring the water to a boil in a 4 quart saucepan. Add the sautéed onions and garlic along with the tomatoes, apples, celery, and coconut. Blend the ginger, sugar, curry powder, flour, salt and pepper with enough cold water to make a paste. Gradually stir the paste into the boiling mixture and simmer, stirring occasionally, for approximately 20 minutes or until the vegetables are tender but still slightly crisp. Add the raw shrimp and cook only 5 minutes longer. Serve over rice, if desired. Serves 6.

POACHED EGGS WITH SHRIMP-SHERRY SAUCE

Sauce

¼ cup butter
4 tablespoons chopped onions
½ cup sliced mushrooms
¼ cup chopped mushrooms
2 tablespoons flour
¾ cup heavy cream
¼ cup sherry or Madeira
¾ cup small shrimp
dash hot pepper sauce
chopped parsley
2 sourdough muffins
4 eggs

Melt butter and sauté onions and mushrooms until moisture is evaporated. Add flour and cook until bubbly. Slowly stir in cream, then sherry. Cook until thick. Stir in shrimp and hot pepper sauce.

Meanwhile, split mufins, butter and toast. Poach eggs and place one egg on each muffin half. Spoon sauce over eggs covering muffins. Sprinkle with parsley. Serves 2-4 either for breakfast or lunch. For special occasions, we would suggest accompanying with a Johannesberg Reisling or pink champagne.

SALISHAN'S STUFFED JUMBO SHRIMP

Prepare stuffing

2 ounces butter
2 ounces onions, peeled, chopped, sautéed in butter
1 ounce shallots, peeled, chopped, sautéed in butter
8 ounces Dungeness crab meat

Season with salt, Tabasco, MSG to taste. Heat thoroughly. Chill. Add parsley, mince in chopper. Adjust seasoning.

If stuffing turns out too soft, add white bread crumbs—to make it more spreadable, add 1 or 2 egg yolks.

Prepare shrimp

Peel, devein, and split (butterfly) large (3-5 per pound) shrimp. (We serve only the largest and use 2 per portion.)

Apply stuffing with a pastry bag in the centerfold. Re-shape shrimp and freeze just enough to handle.

Bread with flour, egg, and white bread crumbs—in that order.

Deep fry or pan fry to brown and finish in oven. Recommended temperature for both—325° to 350°F.

GARLICKY SHRIMP

1 pound medium shrimp, shelled
½ cup melted butter or ¼ cup butter and ¼ cup salad oil
⅛ teaspoon powdered garlic

Combine all ingredients in oven dish and marinate 2-8 hours. Bake in 375°F. oven until firm and pink, about 10 minutes. Serve immediately with crusty rolls to absorb the butter. Serves 3-4.

SHRIMP CLOUD APPETIZERS

1 pound shrimp, chopped
1 egg, lightly beaten
1 teaspoon cornstarch
1 teaspoon sugar
3 ounces water chestnuts, finely chopped
2 green onions, finely sliced

Combine all ingredients and drop by teaspoons into oil preheated to 375°F. Fry until golden brown and drain well on paper towels. Serves 4-8.

SHRIMP AND CANTALOUPE LUNCHEON SALAD

1 pound small shrimp, shelled and cooked
2 small cantaloupes
⅓ cup finely sliced celery
1 cucumber, thinly sliced
1 tablespoon lemon juice
1 cup slivered almonds, toasted

Cut cantaloupes in half and scoop out seeds. Make melon balls. Combine balls with shrimp, celery, cucumber, and lemon juice. Refrigerate.

Just before serving, fill shells with mixture and sprinkle with nuts. Present each diner with cantaloupe half and pass dressing. Serves 4.

DRESSING

Blend together ⅓ cup mayonnaise, ⅓ cup sour cream or unflavored yogurt, 1 tablespoon lemon juice, 1 teaspoon grated lemon peel, and 1 teaspoon Dijon mustard.

SESAME SHRIMP

1 pound medium shrimp, shelled
½ cup toasted sesame seed divided among 3-4 individual sauce dishes
3 tablespoons oil
3 tablespoons lemon juice
⅛ teaspoon garlic powder
1 tablespoon honey, slightly warmed
¼ teaspoon ground ginger

Combine oil, lemon juice, garlic, ginger, and honey in shallow pan. Stir in shrimp and mix to coat. Cover and marinate overnight, stirring frequently.

Drain shrimp. Spread on baking pan and broil, basting with marinade and turning, until pink and firm, about 5-8 minutes.

Divide shrimp among diners, allowing each person to dip in his own dish of sesame seeds. Serves 3-4.

SEAFOOD SALAD

½ pound shrimp, cooked, shelled, and chopped
½ pound crab meat
½ loaf French bread, crusts removed and slices cubed into 20 parts
½ cup sliced green onions
2 hard boiled eggs, chopped
½ cup sliced celery
¼ cup sliced water chestnuts
1½ cups mayonnaise

Combine bread, onions, and eggs; refrigerate overnight to blend flavors. Add shrimp, crab, celery, water chestnuts, and mayonnaise and mix well. Refrigerate 4-5 hours. Serves 6.

SHRIMP AND MUSHROOM RAMEKINS

1 pound shrimp, cooked and shelled
4 tablespoons butter
½ pound mushrooms, sliced
3 tablespoons sliced green onions
3 tablespoons flour
⅛ teaspoon Dijon style mustard
⅔ cup chicken broth
½ cup whipping cream
3 tablespoons sherry

Divide shrimp among 2-3 individual baking dishes and set aside. Melt butter. Add mushrooms and green onions; cook until limp. Add flour and cook until bubbly.

Stir in mustard, chicken broth, and whipping cream. Cook until thickened, stirring constantly. Add sherry and pour sauce over shrimp, dividing among the 2-3 baking dishes.

Bake at 325°F. for 10 minutes or until mixture is heated thoroughly. Serves 2-3.

SHRIMP CREOLE

Cook 2 pounds of broken shrimp in 2 gallons of water. Add salt and dash of Cayenne pepper. Mix in Spanish Sauce. Serve over rice pilaf.

Spanish Sauce

Slice into julienne sections 2 large onions, 2 green peppers, and 1 celery stalk. Sauté until half cooked. Add 2 No. 202 cans of diced tomatoes and 2 of tomato sauce. Bring to boil. Add 3 tablespoons of whole oregano and 3 of sweet basil. Stir in dash of Tabasco sauce and salt and pepper to taste.

SCAMPI FLAMBÉ

Use 5 large, peeled scampi, butterflied and the inside cleaned out.

Heat pan, pour a bit of brandy for flambé effect, then place herb butter into hot pan. While butter is melting, put into it chopped, diced onions, white and green.

Add scampi, after 2 minutes of cooking on both sides, flavor with chablis and a bit of sherry, let simmer, squeeze the juice of a lemon into pan, turn scampi several times for even cooking, then flambé with generous shot of brandy.

Serve on garnished, hot dinner plate.

. . . . SQUID . . . .

Slit the squid's hood in half lengthwise. Lay flat; scrape out and discard interior portions including transparent shell. Peel off speckled membrane from outside of hood. Rinse hood and dry well. One pound of squid hoods in sauce serves 2-4.

SQUID CURLS IN COGNAC SAUCE

1½ pounds squid, hoods only, cut in half crosswise and dried thoroughly
3 tablespoons oil
2 tablespoons cognac
⅓ cup sherry
3 medium tomatoes, coarsely chopped
¼ teaspoon powdered garlic
1 bay leaf
¼ teaspoon dried thyme
⅛ teaspoon cayenne pepper
3 tablespoons butter, cut into chunks

Heat oil and stir-fry squid pieces over high heat until curled and firm. Add cognac and flame. When flames die down, add remaining ingredients and bring to boil. Lower heat, cover, and simmer 45 minutes.

Remove squid pieces to heated platter. Reduce sauce by boiling until thick. Stir in butter chunks until melted and well blended. Pour sauce over squid. Serves 2-3.

RICE WITH SQUID

½ cup long grain rice
1 tablespoon butter
1¼ cups chicken broth
1 pound squid, cleaned, hoods cut into thin rings
3 tablespoons sliced green onions
2 tablespoons butter

Rice

Melt butter in saucepan over medium heat. Add rice and cook, stirring, until rice begins to brown. Add chicken stock, bring to boil, reduce heat, cover and simmer until fluffy or about 20 minutes.

Squid

Melt remaining butter in small pan. Stir in squid and green onions. Cook over low heat until squid is just pink. Stir into rice and serve to 4 people as a side dish.

You'll find this dish even more interesting when paired with grilled steaks and stir-fried vegetables.

STIR-FRIED SQUID WITH VEGETABLES

1 pound squid, hoods only, cut into 1-inch strips
2 tablespoons oil
2 thin slices ginger root, minced
½ cup each sliced celery and green onions
½ cup green peas
⅓ cup chicken broth
½ teaspoon sugar
2 tablespoons soy sauce
1 tablespoon cornstarch
⅛ teaspoon garlic powder

Combine chicken broth, sugar, soy sauce, cornstarch, and garlic powder to form sauce and set aside.

Heat oil and stir-fry minced garlic 1 minute. Add squid pieces and stir-fry 1 minute more. Add vegetables and cook until heated through, 2-5 minutes. Mix in sauce and cook until hot and thick. Serves 2-3.

DEEP-FRIED SQUID

1 pound squid, hoods only, cut into quarters
¾ cup flour
⅓ cup cornstarch
1 teaspoon baking powder
½ teaspoon salt
1 egg, lightly beaten
⅔ cup water
1½ tablespoons oil

Blend together flour, cornstarch, baking powder, and salt. Combine egg, water, and oil; stir into flour mixture until smooth.

Dip squid pieces into batter and deep-fry in oil preheated to 375°F. until golden. Drain on paper towels. Serves 2-3.

STUFFED SQUID IN TOMATO-VEGETABLE SAUCE

1½ pound squid, hoods only, left whole
1 tablespoon butter
1 green onion, sliced
¼ cup chopped mushrooms
½ tablespoon lemon juice
1 pound can whole tomatoes
¼ teaspoond dried thyme
½ cup soft bread crumbs
3 tablespoons oil
¼ cup white dinner wine
½ cup each sliced carrots and celery

Melt butter in small skillet. Add green onion and mushrooms and lightly sauté. Add lemon juice, one whole tomato (coarsely chopped), and thyme. Simmer 5 minutes.

Remove from heat and stir in bread crumbs. Stuff squid loosely, as they will shrink, and secure with toothpick.

Heat oil in skillet and lightly brown squid rolls. Add remaining ingredients and bring to boil. Reduce heat, cover, and simmer 30 minutes.

Remove squid to heated platter and boil down sauce. Pour sauce over squid and serve 4-8. This makes a real conversation-starting hors d'oeuvre.

. . . . . NOTES . . . . .

. . . . . *NOTES* . . . . .

. . . . . *NOTES* . . . . .

Index

About The Authors

The affection the Taylors feel for the Oregon coast dates back to early childhood.

Mary, born in England, moved to the Northern Oregon coast with her parents at a tender age and lived there until young adulthood precipitated a move to Portland to further her education. She developed a fascination with gourmet cooking shortly thereafter which was expanded and broadened during a year's teaching assignment in Brazil. An interest in Oriental and French cuisine developed in the succeeding years. Now, her husband's many and successful fishing exploits demand that preparation of fish and shellfish be given particular attention.

Steve's memories of the coast begin at age five, when his family began vacationing there. It's been his favorite place ever since. In the past several years, an avid interest in the many outdoor activities available there—clam digging, crabbing, hunting and, above all, fishing—has added a new dimension. The coastal streams are his first love, and the wily steelhead his preferred adversary. Winter steelheading in the perpetual, cold drizzle has, he says, brought new meaning to the word "misery". Stoicism is, of course, an integral part of the experience and in reality he wouldn't change a thing about it.

Both Steve and Mary place great importance on the dining experience, and the idea of writing a book dealing with the exciting table fare available on the coast was, as they say, "a natural". The strongly favorable response to the first edition of **Dining on the Oregon Coast** prompted them to publish this thoroughly revised, updated and expanded edition. As with the original, they hope this guide will help others to maximize their enjoyment of this land of many wonders.

The Taylors now reside in the Seattle area, with a home overlooking Poverty Bay on Puget Sound. Weekends often find them on the Oregon coast again, fishing, clamming, exploring, strolling the beaches, breathing the clean salt air and working up an appetite for yet another sample of the bounty of the sea.

The cover shows the Taylors dining in style at a secluded spot on a favorite Northern Oregon beach.